THE LOST ROADS OF WESSEX

Also available in the David & Charles Series

The David & Charles Series

THE LOST ROADS OF WESSEX

C. COCHRANE

UNABRIDGED

PAN BOOKS LTD : LONDON

First published 1969 by David & Charles (Publishers) Ltd.
This edition published 1972 by Pan Books Ltd,
33 Tothill Street, London, SW1.

ISBN 0 330 02991 6

Printed and bound in England by
Hazell Watson and Viney Ltd,
Aylesbury, Bucks

Contents

Illustrations in Photogravure
(between pages 98 and 99)

Introduction

THIS book is a product of the age. Twenty years ago it could not have been written. Twenty years ago the old road maps which are its foundation were still lying, seldom examined, in museums and libraries.

There they still lie, those road maps and route guides, many of them prepared centuries ago, some so rare that there is only a single manuscript drawing. From the mid-1700s large-scale maps were being produced that simply bubble with information, but they are of little practical value in record offices, because a map, to serve its purpose, must be studied and re-studied, compared with other maps, taken out and put to work on the actual site. It is only recently that new photocopy methods have given them back their true, magnificent worth.

Now to many people roads are a constant magnet, with their waywardness and their never-endingness and the sense of eternity about them. In the author's case the magnet exercised its pull from early childhood; on foot and bicycle and horse and car his pursuit of the Wessex byways has never slackened. Rather it became intensified as growing knowledge seemed to give the byways a pattern often more definite than that of the major roads. The reading of whatever histories were available began to suggest that the ancient records fitted more easily into them than into the big highways.

The first real evidence came with a casual glance at one of those small county maps of the 1700s which, in their gay colours and frames, embellish the walls of many a home. It showed the mail-coach roads in thicker outline, and all of a sudden the fact stood out that the route of one of these coach roads was not comparable with the equivalent main road today. From then onwards, with much trial and error, the picture became clearer. In Wessex at any rate a number of what are thought to be old, unchanging trunk roads, are only the creations of the turnpike system that came in some 200 years ago. The earlier systems were quite different.

Once this was learned it became essential to test the whole road structure with the help of the photocopies of maps and documents which can now be obtained for permanent retention. Thanks to the cooperation of those concerned, a library of some 300 large-scale early maps relating to the main Wessex area, bounded roughly by Chichester, London, Oxford and Seaton, was built up, mostly from the British Museum, together with innumerable other records of which the more important are listed in the bibliography.

Thus a fresh survey of these lost main roads became possible by following the maps and route guides – for the most part on site – of the 1600s and 1700s, before the modern turnpikes were contemplated. To relate the survey to its surroundings, contemporary sources have been quoted whenever they could be found, and though some of the authors are famous enough, it is seldom that their writings are encountered in these particular contexts.

The very early ridgeway tracks, and the hard-core Roman roads, have received and continue to receive ample examination from students. The tale here has been taken up at the beginning of English history, with the road system as it would have been met by an incoming Saxon about AD 500, after the Roman departure. It has been carried through to the arrival of the railways and the decline of the stage coach in the first half of the 1800s.

A debt of real gratitude is due to the editor and staff of the *Hampshire Chronicle* in Winchester, who so warmly supported the author's researches in that county, as they have been supporting earlier authors for upwards of 200 years. Though it is here presented in different, expanded form, much of the material on Hampshire has appeared in the *Chronicle* in the recent past; it was the critical yet always encouraging comments of that paper's readers which strengthened confidence to complete the book.

As might be expected, the most complex network is that between the rivers Itchen, Wey and Thames, which represent the growing, and then declining, contacts of the twin capitals Winchester and London. In the attempt to decipher the routes over the uplands that form the watershed of these rivers, which seem to have known at least four road systems, the help of Mrs Olivia Mills of Wield Wood, with her meticulous research of old documents coupled with her spirited argument, was beyond reckoning. It was she who introduced Mr Philip Sheail of Fleet, who drew the maps with such ready perception of their purpose.

The author's wife made everything possible in the manner of the best wives the world over. Without her the job would never have finished. But she deserves the bulk of the credit for another reason, simply that her idea of a pleasant day's outing is not fulfilled by an obsession with old byways and their attendant mud.

C. COCHRANE

Ropley,   *June* 1968
near Alresford,
Hampshire

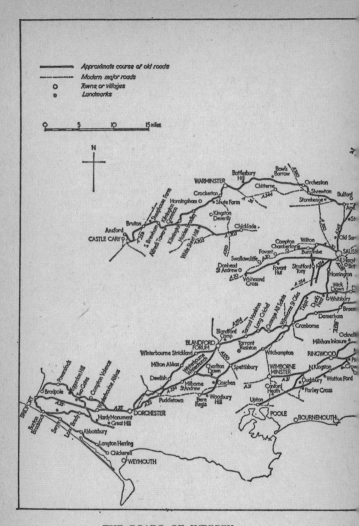

THE ROADS OF WESSEX

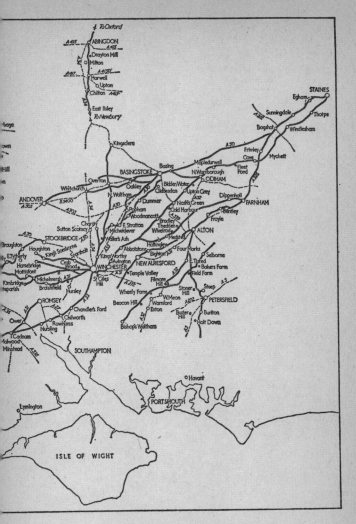

THE ROADS OF WESSEX

THE LOST ROADS OF WESSEX

CHAPTER ONE

The Land's End Road

WINCHESTER TO ST IVES

THE road to Cornwall from the Straits of Dover has as good a claim to antiquity as most. This was acknowledged by the Gough map of about 1360, though the course it showed was not along the original pre-Roman throughway. (It takes one route from Canterbury to Southampton and another from Winchester to St Ives.) The western stretch from Winchester is in fact a continuation of the road from London, running to Kingston, Cobham and Guildford, Farnham, Alton and Alresford and so to Winchester: thence to Salisbury, Shaftesbury, Chard, Honiton, Exeter, Okehampton, Camelford and St Ives; a route that the Ministry of Transport could accept as a reasonable substitute for their A30.

It is notable, at a period in the 1300s when London's supremacy over Winchester might be thought to have become established, that this Great West or Land's End road, as it came to be known, was still routed through the old capital at Winchester rather than the short cut from Basingstoke via Andover to Salisbury such as is followed nowadays and has been for many centuries.

Equally noteworthy is the fact that, even in those comparatively early days, the road from Basingstoke to Winchester was ignored. In this motoring century people have grown up in the assurance that it is part of the premier route from London to Winchester, and since miles of it follow the Roman Silchester road, have assumed that this always was the case. Actually it would seem that most of this particular highway was neglected soon after the Roman

administration was removed. (In all that eight-mile stretch
between Popham and Kings Worthy, there is not a single
village.) It was not brought back to use as a main road till
the turnpike days of the mid-1700s, and even at the height
of the coaching era it failed to become the number one road
from London.

WEST FROM SHAFTESBURY

The ways east of Shaftesbury are treated later in this chapter, but a quick survey of the road's passage west of that
town should be attempted, for though it passes beyond
what most people would regard as Wessex proper, it is a
background route that affects the whole network. And the
strange thing about it is that it seems to have remained
through all its history very much the same as it is today. In
fact, as far as Exeter, its course in 1360 seems to have been
almost a counterpart (except for a slight divergence around
Chard) of that given by Ogilby (Illus. 1), some 300 years
later. There seems to be no firm evidence as to its route in
the years before 1300, for no Roman way has been listed or
located between Salisbury and the southern part of the
Fosse. It would, perhaps, have centred at one time on
Roman Ilchester on both Fosseway and Harroway, the
latter linking with the Roman Salisbury–Mendips road for
its eastern passage; but when the more southerly route
through Salisbury to Chard came into being can only be
guessed. It may have developed to its full length as a
throughway as Christianity re-emerged into Saxon England
and found a local headquarters at Crediton.

Stukeley evidently believed that the earliest road was even
closer to the coast, at Colyford just north of Seaton on the
Fosseway. At Colyford, he wrote, 'was the ancient road
from London to Exeter passing over at Axbridge ... Here
have been many inns and houses, and a considerable town.'
Although a Roman road is thought to have passed here,
Stukeley makes it clear that his town was a later one, with
the corollary that his 'ancient road from London' was not a

continuation of the Roman way through Dorchester, but of the Salisbury–Crewkerne route. In the early 1300s it was of sufficient importance to have been shown as one of the few place-names on the Gough map.

At least, then, the Gough route, by Chard and Honiton, compared very easily with Ogilby's of 1675, which he gave, from Salisbury, as through Shaftesbury, Sherborne, Crewkerne, near Chard, Axminster, Honiton, Exeter and then coastwise through Plymouth and Penzance. This, he assured his readers, was one of the chief roads of the kingdom, and there are some magnificent records to show the realities of West Country travel in those pre-turnpike days; several writers describing what they saw or suffered within a few years of 1700. Conditions then cannot have been greatly different from what they had been from Saxon times onwards, except perhaps that they were at their lowest ever.

Here is Defoe's impression of the road across Salisbury Plain approaching Shaftesbury:

> It has neither house or town in view all the way, and the road which often lyes very broad, and branches off insensibly, might easily cause a traveller to loose his way, but there is a certain never failing assistance upon all these downs for telling a stranger his way, and that is the number of shepherds feeding, or keeping their vast flocks of sheep, which are every where in the way, and who, with a very little pains, a traveller may always speak with.

(The traveller might be none the wiser, for the West Country dialect or 'jouring' was such that he 'cannot understand one half of what they say'.)

Shaftesbury, added Defoe, 'is now a sorry town' and Ogilby continued that 'it is seated on a high hill quite destitute of water, which is brought to them on horses from the foot of the hill' and (what is not so well known) that after the place became a centre of pilgrimage to the tomb of the murdered Saxon king Edward the Martyr, 'his shrine afterwards was so visited by devotists that the town for a time bore his name'.

From Shaftesbury it is clear enough that the line of the present road westwards to Sherborne existed at any rate in Saxon times, the two towns having strong religious ties which extended back to Winchester. Though Roman relics are not prolific in the area, enough have been found to justify an assumption that the route was travelled in the Roman-British period as far as the Fosseway connexion beyond Crewkerne. This would have meant three main westward medieval roads: the southern (Roman coastal defensive) route through Dorchester and Bridport, the more northern Harroway through Basingstoke and Amesbury to join the Fosse near Ilchester, and the central road through Sherborne and Chard. Seekers of the Cornish tin road can use any of these, according to where their theory of the export site leads them.

Nowadays the way westwards from Shaftesbury is by a strange zigzag hill that leads on to Sherborne, with a clumsy turn to Gillingham. It is modern, and the old roads to each place left the town by separate routes, the Sherborne route being the steep hill near the Grosvenor Hotel. The Ogilby road continued through Five Bridges to Sherborne and so, by Babylon Hill to Evill (Yeovil). It may be worth noting that the tradition of Camelot at Cadbury was strong enough in the 1600s for it to be mentioned in Ogilby's comments on Yeovil, which is some distance away and on a different road: 'The ruins of an ancient castle called by the people King Arthur's Palace,' he wrote. He continued along the line of the A30 to Crewkerne, but here the two part company, the A30 running through Chard to Honiton, whilst Ogilby cut south through Street, bypassing Chard, and reached Honiton via Axminster.

This is what Stukeley had to say:

At Petherton Bridge, near South Petherton, was formerly a wooden bridge, but ruinous, where two children were drowned, as they say; whereupon their parents rebuilt it of stone, and caused their effigies to be cut upon a stone which lies at the foot of the bridge ... Beyond this the Foss grows intricate and obscure, from the many collateral roads made through the badness and want of reparation in the true one ... The street of Chard runs directly east and west. Beyond this to Honiton is a very bad road of stones and sand, over brooks, spring-heads and barren down. From the hilltops about Stockland I first had sight of the southern ocean; a most solemn view, a boundless extent of water thrown into a mighty horizontal curve.

And a contribution from Celia Fiennes, who found that the farther her travels took her west, the worse the roads became. Near Plymouth,

Here the roads contract and the lanes are exceedingly narrow and so cover'd up you can see little about, an army might be marching undiscover'd by anybody for when you are on these heights that show a vast country about, you cannot see one road: the wayes now become so difficult that one could scarcely pass by each other, even the single horses, and so dirty in many places and just a track for one horse's feete, and the banks on either side so near, and were they not well secured and mended with stones struck close like a drye wall every where when they discover the bancks to breake and molder down, which else would be in danger of swallowing us the way quite, for on these bancks which are some of them naturall rocks and quarrys, others mended with such stone or slate struck edgeways to secure them, for the quicksetts and trees that grow on these bancks loosen the mold and so it makes molder downs sometimes.

And near Ashburton,

All their carriages here are on the backs of horses with sort of hooks like yoakes upon each side of a good height, which are the receptacles of their goods ... and I cannot see how two such horses can pass each other or indeed in some places how any horse can pass by each other, and yet these are the roads that are all hereabouts.

From Axminster, said Miss Fiennes,

I came to the London road by Chard ... its such an enclose country and narrow lanes you cannot see a bow shott before you ... one night raine put the cattle in the meddows swimming and hinderd us from going to church, the water would have come over the windows of the coach.

Arthur Young was complaining about the narrow West Country roads even after the turnpikes were being made in the latter part of the 1700s. Of the road from Gloucester to Newnham, west of the Severn, he wrote,

... The same stony hard and rough roads miscalled turnpikes; it is all a narrow lane; ruts all the way; they build their wagons with their wheels full three inches nearer to each other than in the eastern counties ... a Norfolk or Suffolk wagon could not stir even in this turnpike road.

At Exeter the Ogilby road kept southward, and the A30 reverts to the route through Okehampton pursued by the map of 1360, beyond the limits of this book. It can however be noted that the Ordnance Survey map of Roman Britain suggests a Roman road through the centre or spine of Cornwall, no doubt related to the tin mines, which seems to be paralleled by the 1360 map. But by Ogilby's 1675 period the tin road had long been forgotten and the interest lay in the coastal towns and their contacts beyond the seas.

THE SALISBURY COMPLEX

In Wessex, unless current excavations at Winchester prove otherwise, Old Sarum is the only important Iron Age hill fort that continued as an important town through Roman to Norman times. It is a remarkable piece of construction, but why the Normans, tough as they might be, should contemplate turning such an ill-favoured and unpopulated site into a cathedral city is beyond understanding. The Saxons, who were not hillsmen, had little regard for the place, and after capturing it in 552 had been content to settle at riverside sites like Harnham and Wilton.

Wilton claims – somewhat improperly – to be the 'ancient capital of Wessex'. It would be on safer ground to style itself the ancient capital of Wiltshire, to which it gave its name. It is curious that of the four counties that are the major constituents of Wessex, three of them take their names, Saxon in origin, from towns other than their present 'capitals' (Wiltshire from Wilton, Somerset from Somerton, Hampshire from Southampton): only Dorset with Dorchester stays firm with the past, and to make sure there is no competition goes right back to its pre-Roman inhabitants, the Durotriges.

The Salisbury locality offers yet another peculiarity which may be unique. Within a few square miles it can provide no less than four one-time capitals – Old Sarum, Wilton, Salisbury itself and Clarendon. For the Norman palace-town of Clarendon (Illus. 11) became, almost from the moment of the Conquest, a political centre where the first representative people's gathering was held in 1086 and where many of the early laws were framed. Nobody seems to have left a record (Leland should have done so in the early 1500s) that from the neighbouring high ground could be seen the towers or pinnacles of all four – surely as rare a sight as was to be found in Europe. Salisbury, the last comer, was carefully sited between the three others, a factor which makes the tracing of earlier road systems extremely difficult. For Salisbury was to become the key traffic magnet for the West Country, with a new road network developed to meet it. And in the task of establishing its antecedents there must be noted at the outset a most strange anomaly, that the historic main route to the west, the A30 through Salisbury, Shaftesbury and Yeovil, had no apparent counterpart in Roman times.

The people who were building the great hilltop walled townships in the centuries preceding the Roman invasion were just as prone as people ever since to petty squabbles and jealousies, but in this part of England their villages – walled or unwalled – were so close to each other that it can only be concluded that they came under the same tribal influence and were in close communication one with another. That being so, an important Iron Age centre such as Old Sarum would have direct trackways leading to its neighbours such as Figsbury to the east, Clearbury and Whitsbury (castle ditches) to the south, Stockton and Swallowcliffe (castle ditches) to the west and Boscombe to the north. These are only a few out of the many sites that might be selected. What is lacking today is the immediate line of Iron Age communication south and west of Old Sarum, because of the later settlement of New Sarum (Salisbury) being developed there. But the line can soon be picked up outside the city, and a guess cannot be far wrong for the Salisbury area.

It is known, for example, that the western Mendips ridgeway through Grovely Wood was in existence, and would be later made into a hard Roman road. It is known that the south-west ridgeway between the Nadder and the Ebble was in use; it was to form the main road till well into the nineteenth century. And for a southern route, to Whitsbury with its junction with the Avon crossing at Charford, either of the old roads which cross the Ebble at Homington and Odstock would provide the line.

The site of Salisbury is always said to have been a marshy one; legend maintains that the sources of the rivers had to be altered to accommodate it. It cannot have been too wet, or neither the city nor its cathedral could have been built there. Moreover it is recorded that when the bridge over the Avon was built at Harnham in the 1200s it superseded a ford. Thus there was a road at Harnham across the site of Salisbury, no doubt leading north to Old Sarum, before the city was ever considered.

The first Ordnance Survey drawings of about 1800 offer a further clue to this north–south route. The byroad from Homington over the Ebble that runs north towards Salisbury passes Wellhouse Farm just before it reaches the main Salisbury–Blandford road (the modern A354). Wellhouse Farm and the nearby cottages were built in this century, but the old map shows a building there marked 'Coldharbour', a name which so far has never failed in pinpointing a road of the walled town or Roman period. This Coldharbour name seems to have passed out of local memory. It lay on the same byroad that Leland claimed to have taken in his ride from Cranborne to Salisbury, though his commentators seem convinced that he really meant the Coombe Bissett road. There is no reason why he should have meant this. Even today the downs are criss-crossed with old trackways, many of them usable. The big-scale maps of the 1700s for Dorset and Wiltshire show how actively they were then kept in use, with Saxon Cranborne taking the place of Iron Age Whitsbury, and the bridge at Downton replacing Charford.

The final support for this Homington road comes from Ogilby's 1675 Oxford–Poole route, which passed through Salisbury and Cranborne. The text and the route map are here unmistakable, showing at Homington a direction to 'Coombe' (Bissett) to the right and 'Odstock' to the left. The bridge at Homington (the present hump-back?) is shown just short of the village and the road continues past 'Tweed Farm' (modern Toyde) with 'Black Warren Lodges' (associated with Roman building) on the other side. Here it joins what was to become the turnpike road from Salisbury to Poole which ran through Coombe Bissett and by Toyde Farm, much of it still being in use as a made-up road.

SALISBURY TO SHAFTESBURY

The Homington route has this other advantage over the Odstock one, that it makes a direct link with the ancient westerly road, the ridgeway that runs from the top of Harnham Hill (the old Blandford road) past the golf links and the Salisbury racecourse, and continues till it rejoins the valley A30 road to Shaftesbury some fourteen miles on. In many ways this is one of the most remarkable stretches of road in England, but its long history is nowadays ignored, and it is high time that it received a pat on its broad, if chilly, back.

As a stretch of road it has no particular name, and for this chapter it is called the Racecourse Way. The authors of *Ancient Trackways of Wessex*, concerned with prehistoric Britain, called it the Salisbury way and the Ordnance map gives it a Saxon slant by naming it 'herepath', though there seems no reason for such a period flavour. It must surely have been known to people in the long, peaceful centuries of Roman Britain. The Roman defensive network provided a series of north–south hard roads that cut up the country into slices – Silchester–Southampton, Silchester–Old Sarum–Dorchester, Cirencester–Ilchester. For trading and other purposes the existing network with some fresh soft-core additions was sufficient. The Harroway running from Dover in Kent to Ilchester in Somerset was one – maybe the chief – of the east–west routes, but there must have been something south of it, and communications along the Sherborne–Shaftesbury–Old Sarum–Winchester line would always have been needed.

About AD 500, when the Saxons were infiltrating into Britain, the south and south-western exits from Old Sarum would have been the hard Roman road to Badbury and Dorchester, crossing the Nadder at Bemerton and the Ebble at Stratford Toney (which in the course of centuries has got distorted from its old name of Stony Stratford). Southwards there would have been the soft road to Whitsbury and Witchampton crossing the Avon at Harnham ford. Then there was the hard Romanized road to the Mendips through Grovely Wood: and finally this soft western race-course ridgeway to Shaftesbury, a continuation probably of an old eastern track that crossed the Avon at Britford, but which in later Iron Age times had found itself joined by a short spur to Old Sarum. This spur, that originally might have run off the Whitsbury road near Harnham, would now perhaps have made use of the newer Badbury road which was somewhat shorter.

In AD 500 the most direct valley route to Shaftesbury from Old Sarum would lie through what would become Wilton, but to avoid the rivers its easiest course would probably have been that which nowadays is part of the Salisbury bypass, branching off at East Harnham, through West Harnham and Netherhampton, across Wilton Park to Burcombe. Such a route might have been used in dry weather, for the traffic along the western road, till the Roman departure, must have been considerable enough to encourage improvements. Would this have been a road used for the export of Cornish tin? If, as some have suggested, part of it was shipped from the Isle of Thanet, it would almost certainly have travelled this way; even the Solent port of Lepe in the New Forest could have been reached by it.

There, then, was the approximate main road network which the West Saxons would have found when, after an interval of many years, they finally took Old Sarum and expanded their settlements westwards. Whatever the future may disclose about the Saxon incursions, it is unlikely to alter a point of view that sees the modern county boundaries between Hampshire and Wiltshire and Dorset as closely representing the state of affairs that existed, in the records of the Anglo-Saxon Chronicle, from 519, when the West Saxons gained the day at Charford and 'obtained the kingdom', till 552, when they put the Britons to flight at Old Sarum. After Charford the West Saxons consolidated their line in Hampshire to hold the lower Avon down to Poole (now Bournemouth) Bay, with a protective outpost at Whitsbury to cover the Charford crossing, and then straightened on a line running northwards which covered Winchester and the Test. Here they maintained themselves, recuperating after their later setbacks, till they amassed strength for the final assault on Old Sarum.

With the more peaceful conditions that seem to have followed in Wessex once Old Sarum had fallen, developments may have been rapid, for here in front of them lay the type of well-watered, fertile land which must have meant much to them after their long dallying in the sandy wastes which cover so much of Surrey and Berkshire and Hampshire. It is a tribute to their staying powers that this dallying extended through generations.

Naturally the rivers were populated on either bank with settlements, and inevitably the site of Wilton, at the confluence of the Wylye and the Nadder, would soon become one of extreme favour. From the 700s it was an important religious centre and the Wessex king had a palace here. Alfred is said to have had the worst of a fight with the Danes in Wilton Park, though why he should be fighting there with Old Sarum so close is hard to understand, unless the Danes had seized it first. The Anglo-Saxon Chronicle is more precise about a similar engagement in 1002, when Wilton was sacked and burnt by the Danes who then proceeded to Old Sarum which they apparently held already.

In Saxon times, therefore, life along this section of the Great West or Land's End road took on an entirely different aspect from what it had known earlier. For one thing, trade for many years must have almost completely dried up, just as the tin export business had faded away in the Roman period when fresh sources were found closer to the Mediterranean markets. But to take its place there were the marching and countermarching along the ridgeway, while the growth of Christianity built up an entirely new form of road usage, with the bishopric first at Wilton and

then at Sherborne, and Shaftesbury almost the most revered
shrine in the country. Was not Edward the Martyr buried
there after his murder at Corfe in Dorset? Did not the
greatest of the Danes, Canute himself, die there? Shaftesbury was indeed a scene of pilgrimage, and Wilton, with the
royal patronage and its own religious houses, was well placed
on the pilgrims' route. At the height of its renown it had
thirteen churches.

WAYS TO WILTON

It is clear from all this that at some early stage of Saxon
progress a direct road must have come into being between
Wilton and Old Sarum, which was still very much in evidence and was to take over the bishopric from Sherborne
in due course, and must certainly have retained its position
as a main traffic centre in western communications, which
flowed through to Winchester, the capital. A glance at the
map will show that the original main roads to Wilton were
those along the river banks, with the western road following the Nadder to Dinton and beyond. The sharp turn at
Barford St Martin for Shaftesbury is clearly a later imposition, and in fact the true road along the valley from
Shaftesbury kept south of the Nadder through Burcombe
and Netherhampton, avoiding Wilton.

It is noticeable how the villages along this Shaftesbury
road, Compton Chamberlayne, Fovant, Swallowcliffe
and the rest, are all sited well north of the present
road. Most probably the first road made its way through
them, and the bypass effect came later. An exactly similar
development can be seen between Alton in Hampshire and
Farnham in Surrey with villages like Holyborne, Froyle
and Bentley, where the old Harrow ridgeway on top of the
hill gave place to the Saxon village route lower down, which
finally moved down from the villages to form a valley
coach road, no doubt to the satisfaction of villages and
travellers alike.

As regards the Old Sarum–Wilton connexion, the present four-mile road is a modern one using the more gradual slopes of Chilhampton Hill. There was a much more direct one of two miles or less, on which the Saxon township may have been built, taking a shorter cut over the hill from Avon Bridge at Stratford sub Castle. Off it was the site of the famous Salisbury tournament in 1194. And so, provided the traveller kept to the village road from Shaftesbury and was prepared to be led along it through Wilton, the arrival of this latter borough was no impediment; in fact his route was rather shorter than it would have been in pre-Wilton days.

What, then, happened to the age-old racecourse ridge-way route from Harnham to Whitesheet which ignored Wilton? There is some evidence that an attempt was made by Wilton to attract its travellers by a track that left the ridgeway south of Burcombe and ran at an angle to Wilton. It will be considered later in this section, but meanwhile it seems clear that in Saxon times – and till the final change in the Norman 1200s – the Great West road was kept open from Old Sarum to Wilton and showed a shortening on its predecessors. But tragedy for Wilton was very close.

The Norman kings from the Conqueror's days were attracted to the Sarum area; so much so that the Saxon site at Wilton was not good enough, and a great new building appeared east of Old Sarum, the palace of Clarendon. It had the added advantage of being closer not only to Winchester, but also to the New Forest, and that without any rivers in between. Then came the ultimate blow – Old Sarum was itself not good enough for the powerful prelates whose see was now centred on the place. Near at hand was this desirable low-lying area, watered in all directions by streams that would simplify living comforts; the king had no objection; and modern Salisbury came into being around 1225. This is what Master Leland wrote down some 300 years later, in an age not confused by day-to-day scares like the present, but when memories were long:

Harnham Bridge was a village long afore the erection of New-Saresbryi ... Licens was get of the king by a Bishop of Saresbyri to turn the kingges highway to New Saresbyri, and to make a mayn bridge for passage over the Avon at Harnham. The chaunging of this way was the totale cause of the ruins of Old-Saresbyri and Wiltoun. For afore this Wilton had 12 paroch chirches or more, and was the hedde town of Wileshir. There was a village at Fisserton over Avon or ever New-Saresbyri was buildid ...

And there is the whole story: the dwellers on the future site of Salisbury, the village that grew up alongside the first ford at Harnham, the village of Fisherton that was to become a suburb of New Sarum and offer its bridge as a further means of attracting traffic from Wilton; perhaps another early settlement by St Martin's Church. Leland does not explain how the highway was turned, and the most likely conclusion is that the road was developed between Fisherton, the western suburb of the new cathedral site (where the County Hotel now stands), and Fugglestone, the eastern suburb of Wilton (where the roundabout is). Such a road would cut off Old Sarum completely, while despite all the hindrances which Wilton was recorded as imposing, nobody would stay there with the major excitements of the new city only two miles away. And then the final blow, the bridge at Harnham, was calculated not only to simplify the passage of travellers along the ridgeway road from Shaftesbury, but also to attract all the southern traffic from Cranborne or Blandford, much of which had hitherto been drawn to Old Sarum direct along the Roman road or via Wilton by the Saxon way or leading there from the Rockbourne area, which meets the Roman road at the Ebble crossing of Stratford Toney.

All that remained was to make the links eastwards with the Hampshire towns and northwards up the Bourne, and the future of Salisbury as a major traffic centre was assured.

Leland was not to know that even a town as far distant as Cranborne (which he found so appealing) would ultimately share the downfall of Wilton and Old Sarum, from the same cause.

But the great advantage of New Salisbury, its plentiful water supply, was to prove a source of trouble. One of the points which always drew the attention of visitors was the method, forestalling Paris by centuries, of conducting the water along both sides of the chief roads so as to form a constant sewage stream. Opinions about its efficiency varied from one extreme to another, and may perhaps have been governed by the season of the year and the changing flow of the streams. Pepys, who was there in June 1668, had a word for the place: 'Come to the George Inn, where lay in a silk bed: and very good diet ... up and down the town, and find it a very brave place. The river goes through every street ... paid the reckoning, which was so exorbitant that I was mad ...'

Jervoise in his *Ancient Bridges of the South of England* goes back much further and is most informative on the crossing at Harnham; how after the bridge was built in 1245 (and for a long time called 'Aylesward') there was continual bickering about responsibility for its maintenance. There was also, it seems, continual bickering about its name, according to the evidence of a book on Cranborne Chase, published in 1841, which quotes record after record from the 1200s onwards, and even shows a so-called certified map of the early 1600s. Without exception, these give Aylesward Bridge as the one at Fisherton. The map also shows Harnham Bridge on its proper site. Usually it is associated (for the arguments hinged round the outer boundaries of the Chase and the correctness or otherwise of collecting tolls) with references to the Avon or Nadder showing that these bounds extended along the river bank from Wilton to Downton; the early bridges being at Bulbridge west of Wilton, Downton south of Salisbury, and the one between these two, 'Aylesward' or 'Aylesford'. This is obviously the Harnham site, but it would be entertaining to know how much trouble was caused in the past by this odd confusion.

After all this it might have been expected that by the 1400s the threat of Wilton would have vanished and the Shaftesbury road would have settled down to a comfortable route along the valley by Compton Chamberlayne, and would have got away from the breezy ridgeway. Around 1400 the main road to London ceased to be routed through Winchester and Farnham, and took the shorter Andover road to Basingstoke. This might have been the time for the Racecourse Way to have quietly dropped out of use; but not a bit of it. The 1400s came and went, the 1500s came and went – and with them the religious pilgrimages that drew the crowds to Shaftesbury. In their place came the new adventurers and traders who were using the western ports to exploit their chances in American waters.

In the 1600s the present Wilton House was built, of which Mr Pepys recorded in 1668, '. . . my Lord Pembroke's house, which we could not see, he being just coming to town: but the situation I do not like, nor the house at present much, it being in a low but rich valley . . .' There is, of course, nothing new in the viewing of stately homes. Miss Fiennes, a few years later, was more fortunate than Pepys, and left a full description, particularly devoted to the almost funfair atmosphere of the gardens:

Two yards off the door of the grotto is several pipes spouts water up to wet the strangers . . . in the middle room the water spouts at the artists pleasure through points all round the room to wet the company . . . they force the water into the roof that descends in a shower of rain . . . in one room it makes the melody of nightingales which engaged the curiosity of the strangers to go in and see, but at the entrance is a line of pipes that washes the spectators, designed for diversion . . .

Neither of these two were travelling the Land's End road, but Ogilby's contemporary survey made clear how the line of the main road was regarded – and it still avoided Wilton and elected the passage along the ridgeway. It is worth a moment's study. Leaving Salisbury, he started off badly by placing Longford House to the right instead of the left of the road, but then 'crossing two vales come on several race posts as the One, Two, Three Mile Posts ...' His text had no further comment or note till '... you come to Whitesheet Hill whose descent is five furlongs'. His route map said little more, other than marking 'the Stand' on the race-course, which must surely be about the oldest map reference in the country to a still-operating course. Evelyn's diary had noted it even earlier, in 1654: 'We returned [to Wilton] by the plain, and 14 mile race [course]. Near this is a pergola or stand, built to view the sports.' Salisbury races and the stand were instituted on a point-to-point basis in the late 1500s.

It is noticeable that, contrary to his usual custom when taking a road through a large town, Ogilby gave not a single direction from Salisbury itself to any other point; along the ridgeway at the end of the racecourse he showed recognizable directions to places on either side such as Wilton. But having come down the descent from White-sheet to the valley road, he gave a backward direction along the valley, in large letters, 'To Salisbury' which his guiding notes marked as a 'different way'. And at this point, in the year 1675, there was no question of this different way being the original village route which would have been the first Saxon road; otherwise it would have run through Donhead St Andrew. But Ogilby has another direction sign northward to 'Donet', quite distinct from his sign to Salis-bury. This valley route is, of course, that part of the A30 distinguished by the carving of regimental crests made in the chalk hillside during the 1914 War. Above them runs the Racecourse Way.

Why should this more comfortable valley route be con-cealed in an age that was just taking to the shaky benefits

of wheeled transport? One look at Whitesheet Hill today
will show what a carriage had to face; it is no fun even for
a horse. Could it be that Ogilby, taking local Salisbury
advice, was reflecting the centuries-old prejudice against the
passage through Wilton which might attract the wayfarer's
custom? From Salisbury, with its gentle approach to the
Racecourse Way, there would be no problem in recommending this ridge route. At the other end, with the sheer
drop (over 400 ft) of Whitesheet looming over the traveller's head, pitted with slithering, steep-sided holloways,
worn into the chalk by thousands of years of usage, even
the toughest would seek a more kindly alternative.

And still the extraordinary Racecourse Way kept going.
Andrews' and Dury's great Wiltshire map of 1773 gives a
picture that seems to have been surveyed just before the
final turnpike road was built at about the same time. At
any rate the milestones, which, although there were excep-
tions erected privately, were in general the proof of a turnpike, did not appear on the valley road but were confined,
on the western routes from Salisbury through Wilton, to
the Stapleford road up the Wylye and the Hindon–Mere
road. Wilton did possess yet another turnpike road which
ran through Ditchampton and then turned westwards below Grovely Wood, taking a course roughtly parallel to the
Hindon road south of it. Not much of it is navigable these
days until it joins the Wylye-Chicklade road A303, some
two miles east of Chicklade, just after it has driven through
what was once the local racecourse.

There was only one other milestone road from Wilton:
that short, angular stretch, mentioned earlier, that ran west
of Wilton Park and branched off to join the Racecourse
Way south of Burcombe.

So the main road in the mid-1700s was still the Racecourse Way, and here Andrews and Dury show a 'mile
tree' on leaving Salisbury, followed by a '2 mile tree', a '3
mile tree' past the 'Salisbury Races' and so on to an '8 mile
tree' just before Chiselbury camp, which was marked with a
bar across the road 'Salisbury Plain Turnpike'. Stukeley, in

1723, wrote, 'the road from Wilton to Shaftesbury, called the Ten mile course . . . a traveller is indebted to Lord Pembroke for reviving the Roman method of placing a numbered stone at every mile, and the living index of a tree to make it more observable'. At seven miles there would have been a chance of refreshment at the Compton Hut, and just after the turnpike ended came the Fovant Hut, where no doubt the westbound traveller would have been advised either to commend his soul to the Almighty or take a side turn to the valley as soon as he could.

Shortly afterwards the valley road must have been strengthened. In a map of 1800 a tollgate had appeared in the valley at the foot of Whitesheet, and the lower road to Barford St Martin was marked with milestones. Yet still the mile trees flourished on the ridgeway as far as Chiselbury, though the tollgate there had been removed. There seems no trace today of those trees or their relics. The Fovant and Compton Huts were marked and of course the racecourse, but that short angled strip of road south of Burcombe had mostly disappeared in enclosed fields. The track to the ridge from Burnbake must still represent it. And so, till the horse was finally abandoned as a means of travel, the Racecourse Way continued to offer its facilities, now thousands of years old. By the 1800s the road and coaching guides were in full spate. Here is the most famous of them, Paterson's. In its fourteenth edition of 1808, which was obviously some years out of date, the road ran from Salisbury to Fugglestone, Wilton and on by Compton Chamberlayne to the turnpike gate at the foot of Whitesheet Hill. At Wilton there was a side direction to the left, showing the alternative road to Whitesheet, and there was also a note that you could travel the whole ridgeway route from Harnham to the racecourse.

Finally there is the very last edition, the eighteenth, published in 1829 but with issues up to 1841, which actually shows the new railroads running to Bristol and Southampton. The description of the London–Exeter coach road takes it through Salisbury, Fugglestone, through the north

of Wilton so as deliberately to bypass the loop on which
the little town stands, and thus to the Whitesheet turnpike
gate. Here appear a whole host of minor directions, pointing to Whitesheet Hill 'To Salisbury, by Fovant Hut and
Wilton, 14¾ m, and, by Fovant Hut and Harnham Hill,
14¼ m'. This compares with the fourteen and three-
quarters miles given for the valley road. There is a note
stating that the Fovant Hut route is 'for travellers on horseback'.

WINCHESTER TO SALISBURY

The River Test makes a wide arc across Hampshire, de-
manding recognition by any traveller westwards. Pre-
Roman peoples used a downstream crossing at Kimbridge
near Mottisfont and a central one at Stockbridge (late
Stoke), but avoided a major east–west crossing upstream
by taking their trunk road, the Harroway, north of the
river.

Roman engineers met it in forthright fashion, downstream at Nursling on the Poole Harbour road, centrally at
Horsebridge, which was probably a ford of long standing,
and upstream at Bransbury Common on the Cirencester
road which was once called the Icknield Way. Later ages
made Redbridge and Romsey their main lower crossings,
with Stockbridge and Whitchurch higher up.

Other than Stockbridge, the earlier routes have either
vanished or ceased to be important, a fact of peculiar significance in the case of Horsebridge, which offers a direct
western road from Winchester that no subsequent alternative could better. It can only be a matter for regret that
this fine Roman throughway is no longer open, for though
minor local sections are still in use, what must at one time
have been a straightforward arrangement of causeway and
bridge over the Test has long since disappeared, to be replaced by a clumsy series of diversions around Horsebridge
and Houghton.

Stukeley's description of 1723 deserves notice. The

Roman way from Old Sarum to Winchester, he claimed, 'has never yet been observed'. North of Clarendon

> On the whole length of Farley Common it is very con-
> spicuous, made of hard matter dug up all along on both
> sides; then ascends the hills at Winterslow; then through
> Buckholt Forest, where with good heed the course of it
> may be followed, though through byways, pastures,
> woods and hedges; sometimes running off the length,
> sometimes crossing it; a little north of West Titherley it
> goes close by a farmhouse and large barn upon a rising
> ground, and at the edge of a wood (Buckholt Farm) ...

The Roman road continued along the ridge

> here called the Causeway, to the river at Bossington,
> though sometimes intercepted by cornfields, where the
> common road goes about, and then falls into it again:
> it passes over the river at Bossington, then marches
> directly to Winchester west gate.

The route so carefully followed was not dissimilar to that which can be followed today, with the 'common road' breaking away and then returning. There was no suggestion by Stukeley that it was in active use as a throughway, and presumably it had no means of crossing the Test even by ford.

It is said that the piles of the Roman bridge were found when the Andover Canal was being dug near Horsebridge lock (Illus. 2). At about the same time, in 1783, it was at Bossington, west of the river, that one of the most tantalizing of Roman roadside relics was turned up: a pig of Mendip lead, dated back to AD 60, which was so obviously destined for export. But which way was it going? Across the Test to Winchester? Or downstream to Lepe or Nursling? It could have told so much, that pig – as its fellow may yet, should one appear nearer the coast. The finding of another pig on this route near Bruton in Somerset is recorded in Chapter 6, section 'Whitesheet Hill'.

In due course came the Saxons, who established a hamlet near the old Roman camp at Ashley, east of the crossing, but tended to start afresh with settlements along the river bank. On the western side they seem to have deliberately rejected the Roman way for an almost parallel road that runs along the Wallop brook to Broughton.

Early Norman reaction looks to have been quite different, for there must have been powerful reasons for maintaining, or reviving, the Roman route to Old Sarum, with three key sites being developed in Wiltshire south of it – Clarendon Palace, the market town of Downton, and eventually Salisbury itself (New Sarum). If the old bridge at Horsebridge had collapsed it would have been repaired, or some alternative brought into use. First of the new enterprises, soon after the 1066 landing, had been the great palace at Clarendon which must surely have been reached from the Roman highway. A direct route between road and palace, by Winterslow Common and Pitton, is clear on old maps, though in those unsettled Norman times no defenceless building such as Clarendon would have been contemplated without the certainty of protection by troops at Old Sarum, two miles away, which again depended on the Roman road system.

But while the comforts of the palace and the thrills of its great hunting woods of Clarendon and Buckholt were being enjoyed west of the river, the same thing on a slightly smaller scale was happening east of it, in what came to be known as 'John o' Gaunt's Park'. In fact the Kings Somborne manor with the forest of West Bere had been royal property at Domesday, but in addition a Norman castle was built about 1200 at Ashley, the only purpose of which would have been to protect the Roman highway. There is perhaps a link here with the graves of numerous early Norman malefactors (poachers?) whose decapitated bodies have been found on both sides of the river at Stockbridge.

A Norman king, therefore, could hunt his way from

Winchester to Clarendon along the line of the old Roman road, with full military protection and excellent halfway quarters. Such a king was John, who in the early 1200s was certainly savouring the pleasures of the route. What is so curious is that at exactly the same time Stockbridge was being developed as a market town; the fortifying of Ashley on the royal Roman road coincided with the expansion of Stockbridge on the commerical Norman one – which was perhaps a shrewd form of pro-Stockbridge propaganda.

At any rate, by the end of the 1200s another hunting king, Edward I, is recorded as making the Clarendon–Winchester journey via Stockbridge, and, though that may be slight evidence, the course of events does support a decline of the Roman road from the 1300s onwards, perhaps coincident with the main London road being routed through Andover, not Winchester. This decline would have spread backwards from the river, after the bridge at Horse-bridge fell into disrepair. On the eastern side the road would have had to journey upstream to find the Stock-bridge crossing. (Stockbridge was known as 'The Street of Kings Somborne'.) It would not be long before a more direct Stockbridge–Winchester route, on the lines of the present one through Weeke, became recognized.

West of the Test the Stockbridge link with the Roman road shows clearly on old maps; it ran on a diagonal through Broughton to a junction near the county boundary beyond Buckholt Farm. This in turn was replaced by the Salisbury route via Lopcombe Corner which is followed today.

Firm support for this prolonged usage of the Roman road, in whole or part, comes from the Gough map of Britain of about 1360, which gives the main western road to London as being routed through Salisbury, Winchester, Alton and Farnham. When the next clues are available in the early 1500s the Salisbury–Andover–Basingstoke route had become the main London road, but never, until this present motoring century, was the Salisbury–Stockbridge–Basingstoke road regarded as the major highway.

All this conforms with medieval economic developments. The 1200s were times of deliberate commercial expansion, which in Wessex was fostered by bishops as well as kings. It centred on sheep production and wool treatment, much of it for export, with Winchester a key centre. The encouragement of Stockbridge as a market and transport town, which was contemporary in the early 1200s with the encouragement of other Wessex markets like Downton and Hindon, New Alresford and Overton, was probably aimed at strengthening communications between the all-important centres of the wool trade.

The Stockbridge crossing was in fact a commercial one which gradually took over all types of traffic as the wars and plagues and the changing habits of the wealthy in the 1300s introduced a decline in the sporting and economic affairs of the region that was to affect it for centuries.

There is one further factor about Stockbridge which would help its popularity – the open plains that led to it were of greater appeal to the traveller than the dense forest lands to the south. It was these same forests, West Bere and Buckholt and Clarendon, which so delighted the hunting Norman kings and resulted in the continued maintenance of the old road that pierced them. Even as late as Leland's time in the early 1500s they were of considerable dimensions, and for much of his journey from Salisbury to Stockbridge along the present route he had Buckholt wood well in sight. It was 'a great thing, where in times past by likelihood hath been a chase for deer'. By contrast his own route, almost all the way from Salisbury to Winchester, lay 'by champain ground barren of wood, with the soil of white clay and chalk'.

BASINGSTOKE TO SALISBURY

In the mid-1300s, as has been shown, there was still enough prestige clinging to Winchester for the recognized London–Land's End road to be routed through it. So long as England was holding some French possessions in direct contact

with the Solent, the arms and the trade handled by the
city would support the case. By the mid-1400s it had
vanished. France and the Channel had had their day; sea-
men in the western ports were seeking wider horizons; for
help they looked to London. It must have been about then
that an ostler in a Salisbury inn said to one of his regulars,
'You know, if you are in a hurry to get to London, there is a
quicker way than through Winchester. You will have to ask
as you go along, but start on the Andover road, and then
they say there is a place called something like Basingstoke.'

Independent corroboration is provided by the statistical
evidence gathered by Professor Hoskins. In 1334, on a
tax quota basis, Salisbury was the 9th most important town,
with Winchester 17th and Southampton 18th. In 1377 (tax-
payers) Salisbury was 6th, Winchester 29th, Southampton
34th. By 1523 (subsidy payments) Salisbury was still 6th,
Southampton 23rd, but Winchester 37th.

It is an anomaly that in Salisbury, a city of no particular
antiquity, so many of the inns are genuine medieval speci-
mens, while neighbouring and much older sites have
modern buildings. Without doubt some of the oldest sites
in England must stand in Wessex, going back a thousand
years or more. To name a few: around Lymington, at
Stoney Cross and Fritham in the New Forest; Winchester
itself, Alton and the crossing of the Wey, Wickham, Cranborne and Wareham, Wallingford and Axminster. Surely
some existing houses must be much earlier than anything
that is attributed to them? The age of inns is an intriguing
study, important for road history. A good deal has been
learnt in recent years, and all the time the dating of inns,
often under different names, is being shown to be earlier
than had been thought. Nevertheless Thomas Burke's
English Inn (1931) gave a list of twenty-two inns dated
from 795 to 1583, of which only two were located in Wessex.

There is no written evidence in the 1400s, but by 1541
the earliest road book appeared (rather in advance of the
maps) which gave the Land's End–London route as branch-

ing from Salisbury to Andover, Basingstoke, Hartford
Bridge, Bagshot and Staines. Basingstoke had at last taken
up its geographical position as road centre. It is an odd
reflection that the very first major road to the west, the
Harroway, skirted the fringes of Basingstoke on its journey
from Dover; that the next road system, the Roman, was
based on Silchester, again bypassing Basingstoke; then followed the period when Winchester was the centre; and
only at the fourth reshuffling did Basingstoke assume its
natural place.

Connexions between Basingstoke and Salisbury must be
almost as old as the hills which surround them, with the
fairground at Weyhill as strong a focus as its Winchester
counterpart of St Giles. From Basingstoke to Andover the
earliest route would have been the Harroway north of the
river. When the Saxon villages came to be laid out along
the Test, they were probably approached from the Harroway
since the original sites seem to have been on the north
bank. The later road south of the river kept well up the hillside and can still be found in places, as at Overton. It only
seems to have disappeared within the last 150 years, with
the present riverside road B3400 slowly taking the traffic.

The one doubtful stretch is for a short distance west of
Basingstoke, near Oakley. By the 1750s the lower road
here and at Andover was already turnpiked, but probably
not all the way, so that Isaac Taylor's contemporary map
looks somewhat jumpy. Earlier than that it may perhaps
have branched to this lost upper road through what is now
enclosed parkland at Oakley and Ash. Ogilby's route ran
some four and a half miles between Oakley and Ash
against the present two miles. He went up and down
hill through a village called in the scroll 'Tetherton'
and in his notes 'Setherton'. This can only fit the
picture if translated as Jane Austen's village of Steventon, which is well up the hill, away from the present lower
road.

But the Harroway (Illus. 4) itself was never discon-
tinued in this part of the country and it is worth following.

It is easy to find just north of Overton where it runs roughly parallel to the railway line, towards Clarken Green. In the early 1700s this is the road the traveller would have taken from Overton church, joining the Whitchurch–Basingstoke road at what is now the Beach Arms at Oakley. A left turn here on the main B3400 towards Basingstoke will find the Harroway continuing as the second turning on the right after the railway bridge. Students of pre-Roman trackways have long suspected that the two loops of the Harroway met near this point, and the evidence from Ogilby's survey of 1675 is most convincing. He showed two ways coming together so that their junction would be a matter of yards from the line of the main road. The line of the lane nearest Basingstoke is obviously the best-known route of the Harroway, coming from Upton Grey.

On this Ogilby scroll map this lane was marked 'to Skippord's Inne' with no mention of town or village. The tracing of this inn illustrates earlier comments on the difficulty of dating these sites owing to name changes and rebuilding. A motorist along the Basingstoke bypass will come to the road leading to Cliddesden and Preston Candover. Just on the junction stands Skippetts House along a side lane which is in fact a part of the old Harroway, and here continues as Viables Lane. By it is the Golden Lion Inn that was largely rebuilt about the time the bypass was made in the 1930s. Last century it was the Lion Inn, by Skippers Farm. In the 1700s it was the Half Way Inn. As Skippord's Inn, recorded by Ogilby in the 1600s, it was clearly of consequence. It does in fact stand roughly halfway between two Harroway towns, Farnham and Whitchurch, perhaps a day's journey apart. And between Oakley and the Basingstoke bypass there is still a clue to the old use of this road; as it goes through Kempshott, and the site of the old Basingstoke racecourse, it is known as Pack Lane.

Skippord's Inn, now the Golden Lion, has survived the Basingstoke bypass. If current plans mature it will shortly be sandwiched on the other side by another new road, the London–Basingstoke motorway M3.

BAGSHOT TO BASINGSTOKE

The London end of the Land's End road, between London and Bagshot, was shared with the London–Southampton road (see Chapter 4) from a date which may have been early Tudor, say the mid-1500s. That does not mean, of course, that no road lay open before then between Andover or Basingstoke and London, but perhaps there was no recognized main road and perhaps it did not go the same way.

A good reason for a different route, that of comfort, is given by the large-scale Ordnance drawing of about 1806 which shows the country just after the Enclosures Acts had taken effect, with all the cultivated field boundaries marked on it. It presented a most striking picture of the Berkshire–Hampshire–Surrey borders as they must have appeared for all the preceding centuries, a picture of a kindly, fertile land with streams like the Loddon and the Whitewater and the Blackwater running northward. But this pleasant paradise came to a sudden end. From Thatchers Ford near Swallowfield in Berkshire all the way down to Farnham in Surrey stretched a great open wasteland – Bramshill and Eversley commons, Yateley Heath (which became Hartford Bridge Flats), Crookham and Aldershot commons. There was only one shallow, enclosed-field, fertile section which bridged this desert, from Elvetham near Hartley Wintney, north of Fleet Pond, through Bramshot to Cove; and even now, with all the urban growth of the 1900s, the sudden greenness of that tiny Bramshot area stands out like an oasis.

A traveller eastwards from Basingstoke (or Old Basing) who followed the lie of the land with no intention of reaching London, would naturally pursue a line leading towards Odiham; and if the urge to reach London came upon him he would break away from this line somewhere between Odiham and Hook, and to avoid the desert would follow this course by Elvetham north of Fleet Pond towards

Farnborough or Frimley. What seems likely is that during medieval times a recognized route linking Basingstoke and Odiham led north-eastwards, towards London though running south of the present London road, and joining an old way from Winchester to the Thames. As the waning of Winchester coincided with the need to strengthen direct communication between London and the west, so a new route was hammered out from Basingstoke, perhaps choosing Hartford Bridge Flats as being higher and drier than the peat bogs around Fleet Pond. Bagshot, already a halting-place on the Windsor–Farnham road, would be the obvious goal.

Hartley Row, which grew up as an accommodation centre, is clearly the child of Hartley Wintney, which was not on the modern main road. Hartford Bridge takes its mis-spelt name from the Earl of Hertford, who obtained possession of Elvetham after the dissolution in 1536. There must have been good reason for a mere bridge to be included in those road books of the 1500–1600s which otherwise give only the main towns. Perhaps it was the last link in the new road, its name symbolizing the fact that commerce and transport were no longer controlled by the Church but had passed to the laity.

Early confirmation of the route, though without its details, came from a particularly gruesome West Country murderer, one Lord Stourton. Tried in London in the mid-1500s, he was sentenced to be hanged in Salisbury, to which it is recorded that he travelled by Staines and Basingstoke.

It would be helpful to establish the dates of inns in the Hartley Row area. The most picture-book inn of that locality, the Raven near Hook, has been a private house for many a year. Hartford Bridge Flats, where the big modern Ely Hotel was built on the site of a smaller inn, was traversed, probably in a north–south direction, in pre-Roman days. Some 200 years ago the main road there ran along a loopway. On its southern side stood a Watch House which was not connected, as it would be today, with aircraft or heath-fire spotting, but more likely with highwaymen. To point the moral, a gallows called Dead Post stood nearby.

The course between Bagshot and Basingstoke thus became that of the A30, except that for a long time it made a slight detour through the village of Newnham.

CHAPTER TWO

Crossing the Test

WINCHESTER TO KIMBRIDGE

WESTWARD from Winchester there have been three main crossing-places of the River Test. With the disused Roman Horsebridge crossing as a centre, the present Stockbridge crossing is just about as far upstream as is, downstream, the old crossing near Kimbridge, used by the pre-Roman ridgeway route. This is one of those early ways whose course can be regarded as fairly clearly established, since the lie of the land makes it so. From its eastward crossing of the Itchen, it left the hill above Winchester roughly along the line of the future Roman Old Sarum road, but then cut at a south-western angle by Farley Mount towards Michelmersh and Kimbridge. Once over the Test it rose again to the ridge south of the Lockerley–West Grimstead valley, along to the National Trust area of Pepperbox Hill. Here it forked off to Redlynch and a crossing of the Avon at Charford, near Downton.

For how long did it serve a purpose? There is appreciable evidence that it, or something like it, was in use well into medieval times, and the route that developed from it is still distinct and usable.

According to the Anglo-Saxon Chronicle – which on this point there seems no reason to reject – it was at Charford (Illus. 7) that the Saxon forces under Cerdic defeated the British in the year 519 and 'from that day on the princes of the West Saxons have reigned'. An interpretation of the conflict is that it enabled the Saxons to gain control of this main road from the west to Winchester together with the Roman Old Sarum road slightly north of it, to cut off

British reinforcements and thus to take Winchester and claim the kingdom.

With Charford offering one of the best crossings of the Avon, it was natural for Downton to develop nearby and be a place of some consequence, which the bishops of Winchester in due course appreciated to the extent that it became one of their possessions and residences. They also owned Hindon to the west of Wilton, the first Wiltshire capital, and expanded both Downton and Hinton as market towns about the year 1200. Their other great property outside their own diocese to the west was Taunton, and all these three towns were on a line of road from Winchester.

It is reasonable, therefore, to expect a throughway to grow up between Winchester and Downton which would have originated in the pre-Roman trackway along which the royal throne of England was first established; and then to find the throughway seeking passage on lower ground, based on the subsequent village or hamlet settlements. This seems to be exactly what did happen and a modern map (ignoring the different road colourings) will disclose a counterpart to the north-western Winchester–Stockbridge road in a south-western Winchester–Kimbridge one. The only alteration is that the Stockbridge road has long since been straightened out, bypassing the villages, since its crossing of the Test has become more and more important for a passage to the whole of the West Country from London; while the Kimbridge route long ago became a minor one when Winchester ceased to be a national road centre for the west.

For evidence of the earliest ridgeway route, settlements along its line from Winchester can still be traced in three village churches which actually survive – Farley, Eldon and Michelmersh – and the remains of a chapel at Manor Farm on the outskirts of Michelmersh. Nowadays the direct link with Winchester is broken and it is a somewhat roundabout journey to reach any of them. A hundred years ago Eldon was said to be the smallest parish in Hampshire with a population of eleven. Its church, with outward appearance now beautifully restored after centuries of misuse, is to be seen in the farm precincts, between house and lane.

Here, then, was the line of the first approach to the Test crossing by Kimbridge, and a map will confirm how close these hamlets were sited on one side or the other to a moderately straight pre-Roman trackway. But soon, and certainly by Norman times, the next stage would have developed, avoiding the ridge of the downland. It followed what is now the Winchester–Romsey road A31 for a few miles to a point between Pitt and Hursley which is marked Standon on the map; and to get the picture of events it is perhaps simplest to work backwards from the 1700s, when the great turnpike road was projected from Popham Lane near Basingstoke to Longham near Poole in Dorset, through Winchester, Romsey and Ringwood.

At a meeting at the King's Head, Hursley, on June 4th, 1759 (most of these turnpike trust proceedings took place in the local inn) the trustees agreed to erect a toll-house and gate at Standon, with a further house covering two side gates in Port Lane and Collins Lane. Having all these toll-gates in the one village was a most unusual process, but the reason for the Port Lane gate (the lane alongside the inn opposite Hursley church) was that it offered – and still does – an alternative 'short cut' to Winchester. It was probably the first Winchester–Hursley route, running parallel to the later A31, and up on the downs near Winchester it passed that old enclosure, thought by some to be Roman, called Oliver Cromwell's Battery. At its Hursley end Port Lane was once connected with the Itchen through Compton and Twyford, where the 'Salisbury road' was a recognized route and must have come this way.

At Standon recent roadwork has smoothed out the corners, but the map still shows how the A31 from Winchester, if continuing a straight course, would run up the hill towards Braishfield instead of swinging left to Hursley. It also shows that the other lane here, signposted Farley and Sparsholt, is on a straight line with the A31 after it bends towards Hursley, and is in fact in line with the road that continues beyond Hursley (B3043) to Chandlers Ford and Southampton. The main road A31 is really a hotch-potch.

So here was once a form of crossroads with one branch running from Winchester up this Braishfield Lane, and the other from Southampton up to Sparsholt and Stockbridge. Thus the route from the north to Southampton could bypass Winchester on the west just as it did on the east by the Alresford–Twyford road. All this is confirmed in the Ogilby 1675 survey – before the turnpike changes – where the way to Sparsholt was marked 'to Andover', while that through Hursley was marked 'to Hampton' (Southampton); Port Lane was marked 'to Winchester' and the Braishfield road was marked 'to Romsey'. At that time the A31 road that forks right for Romsey beyond Hursley was an alternative, a wandering mud track called Ratlake Lane.

The picture of the Winchester road to Kimbridge is thus apparent, as it emerged in medieval days once the ridgeway route was going out of favour. The road ran to this Standon crossways, continued up Braishfield lane, and towards the top of the hill, on the left, can be seen the reason. The green earthworks there are the remains of Merdon, the Iron Age fortress that became a royal Saxon resort and in turn a great Norman castle. To the Iron Age peoples Merdon was the southern counterpart of Woolbury on the northern side of the Winchester–Old Sarum ridge. In Norman days it perhaps corresponded to Ashley across the ridge. Not so long ago, it is said, there were deep trackways near Merdon that must have connected these cross-ridge points.

Once more the map will show, as it continues along this lane to Braishfield, that even today the line from Winchester leads to the old Test crossing at Kimbridge. Many of the more direct lanes, probably including the one that led to the heart of Romsey, have now gone out of use or were abolished in the enclosure period, but it is still a simple journey to Timsbury or Michelmersh and the Bear and Ragged Staff Inn, which leads to Kimbridge. The Normans, ever on the lookout for a good site on an old road, built Mottisfont Abbey nearby, which made a pleasant resting-place. And

the traveller knew that across the Test he had a good valley
open to him which avoided the old ridgeway till the last possible moment at Pepperbox Hill; the valley that had proved
so popular with farmers from Roman days onwards, along
by Lockerley and East and West Dean: the route that led
to Downton and (when it was built) to Salisbury.

THE LUNWAY

Of the various apparently pre-Roman trackways that memo-
rialize man's passage through Wessex, the Lunway, which
crossed the Test by Stockbridge, has been magnified out of
all proportion to its merits. The reason is that, like many
old roads, it once bore a name or, to make the point more
accurately, a section of it once bore a name; this section
then became a quite famous thoroughfare till early in this
century; and the name by that time had been perpetuated
in a drovers' inn which is now a well-known motorists'
port-of-call, though it really has nothing to do with the Lunway.

The Lunway track became famous because it formed the
northern boundary on Worthy Down of the fashionable
Winchester racecourse, which was in use at least from the
1750s and continued for some 150 years. People in South
Wonston remember it to this day, and how the racegoers
proceeded along the Lunway in coach or trap, from the junction with the main Winchester–Basingstoke road, where the
Lunways Inn stands.

The inn, which might equally have been named the
Drovers', or for that matter the Racecourse, was built towards the end of the 1700s following the construction of the
Winchester–Basingstoke turnpike, now the A33. The other
half of the crossroads on which it stands (though only the
eastern half of it is a made-up road these days) was a great
medieval droveway called the Alresford Drove, coming
from the Weyhill–Barton Stacey direction and linking with
the Alresford and Odiham markets. One of these links bi-
secting the downs between Preston Candover and Wield is

still called the Oxdrove, though sheepway might have been more accurate.

The track called the Lunway came, it is said, from Old Sarum or thereabouts and took a line towards Stockbridge on which the modern road via Lopcombe Corner is based. Such a track could well have existed in pre-Roman times and continued as a subsidiary to the new hard Roman highway from Old Sarum to Winchester. The crossing at Stockbridge seems always to have attracted traffic. On the eastern side of Stockbridge the track ran almost due east – well north of Crawley – towards the future racecourse at the future South Wonston, and it is hereabouts that it received its name.

Between Crawley and the site of the Lunways Inn it is mentioned in two Saxon charters as the 'Lundun' way and the 'Lundun herepath', which latter means more particularly an army road. There seems no trace of this 'Lundun' name elsewhere than in this short stretch of five miles, and it is rather flimsy evidence on which to reconstruct a prehistoric road from Old Sarum to London, as has been seriously proposed. London was a place of no particular significance until Roman times, while as regards its use in a Hampshire charter it may be asked how many West Saxons, the hub of whose life was Winchester, had ever heard of London in Middlesex, let alone connecting it with a local road. To this day there is no London road from Winchester; there is a choice between the Alresford road and the Worthy road.

The word 'London' is one of the commonest place-names in England – in Hampshire alone it can be met from Silchester in the north to Lyndhurst in the south. Its origin is uncertain, though it has been suggested that in Wessex it could be just Lun (commonplace or well-used) and Dun (a down). Thus lunway or Lundun-way would refer to a popular track over the downs, with herepath confirming that, being a pre-Saxon track, it avoided Saxon villages and was thus suited to the military.

This London theory – which has only recently been

advanced but has gained adherents – appears to have been put forward as a fact by a distinguished archaeologist (since deceased) who in the 1930s was writing:

> ... the Lunway is an old prehistoric track from Stockbridge and the west. It crosses the Winchester–Basingstoke road at the Lunways Inn ... crosses the Candover stream at Totford, and on by the sheepway and maulthway to London ...

His words were accepted, and so the tale was repeated down to the 1960s when later research and field workers stated, '... it was once on a direct route to London ... afterwards used by the Saxons as part of a throughway to London from the west ...' Why their route should be so circuitous, and why it should cut out the Saxon route from Winchester to London, is not explained.

The use of the term maulthway (there is a suggestion that it means mutton or sheep) is found in a short stretch of lane near Crondall on the Hampshire/Surrey border, many miles from Totford, and again on Chobham Ridges near Bagshot in Surrey. The link between these disconnected stretches, and how they reach London, has not been given, and the writers in the 1960s are content to leave the problem at Totford with the remark that the road 'could have joined the harroway', which is an east–west route that might lead back towards Old Sarum but certainly not to London.

What else has been said about the Lunway? The writers of 1965 pointed out that at South Wonston it keeps on a very straight length, and thought that it may have been Romanized to lead to some unknown Roman site. This straight stretch is that alongside the old racecourse, and older maps (for example, the large-scale original Ordnance Survey drawings of about 1805) show that the track at that time gave no suspicion of straightness. So the 'Romanized' stretch was either a creation of last century connected with improvements to the racecourse, or of this, perhaps connected with the aerodrome that took its place.

It is slightly east of this point that the Lunway disappears. It reaches the Stoke Charity road to Winchester and stops dead, so that to continue eastwards it is necessary to turn left up the Stoke Charity road for some three-quarters of a mile and then right, along the droveway that leads to the Lunways Inn. The Lunway used to continue rather farther east to the more important north–south highway through Weston near Micheldever to Winchester, but the result was the same. This stretch of the highway has now vanished. What happened to the Lunway is clear enough – it was a victim of alcohol.

As has been said, the Lunways Inn was built towards the end of the 1700s when the new turnpike, now the A33, was made. It was built on the cross ways with the Barton Stacey–Alresford drove, which must have been the important route, not the Lunway to its south. The Lunway succumbed to the lure and drifted up to participate; it has lost its bearings ever since. It is worth noting that the inn from its earliest days was called Lunways in the plural, which suggests that the term had a more general application and might have been given to both routes. It could well be that, as the original Lunway ceased to act as a drove, its western end towards Stockbridge was altered to meet the more northerly Alresford drove, which thus acquired the Lunway name. Older inhabitants to this day call the Alresford drove the Lunway.

It is here that the London school, which cannot have made a close study of old maps, becomes active. It has not noted how the route changed with the arrival of the inn, and so follows a parish boundary from the Lunway's vanishing point up to the inn. Older maps, which show the boundaries by hundreds, not parishes, agree that the pre-inn droveway was the southern boundary of Micheldever Hundred, and that there was a wedge of Buddlesgate Hundred between that and the Lunway, which along by the racecourse till its disappearance was a boundary of Barton Stacey Hundred.

The two roads, now combined, travel east of the inn to a fork about a mile away. The right branch of this fork would have been that by which the Barton Stacey droveway justified its name as the Alresford drove and swung towards the Itchen. It would also have joined with the course of the Lunway before it was drawn from the paths of rectitude. The parish boundary supports all this by travelling with the right-hand fork, away from London. So the London school decided that the boundary has played its part, and that the 'true' Lunway kept left and northerly, to reach Totford with the aid of some very sharp bends in most tracklike manner.

At Totford, running past the Woolpack Inn, a building of the early 1800s, there is certainly an old track currently called the Oxdrove; it is the same one which the London theorists would use for their journey, though none of them has disclosed what happened when it finishes its course over Preston Down. Old maps show that from the late 1500s, when there is a most meticulous estate map, to the early 1800s, with the careful enclosure award maps, the track led round towards Chilton Candover or to the open downs, where it ceased to be recognizable. From the mid-1700s all this part of Hampshire was being remodelled by the new enclosures, and what had been an ocean of downland became contracted to a narrow channel. Then the roads had to be laid down where no recognized highway existed, and this Oxdrove is known to have been, at any rate in part, a creation of that time, with its inn, the Bangor.

Fortunately there is some further first-hand evidence in John Duthie's uncompleted *Sketches of Hampshire*, published in 1839. Duthie was a leading county magnate, a pioneer farmer and one who knew the country intimately, living nearby at Ropley. It is not impossible that the London theory started with a careless misreading or misquoting of what he wrote, which could turn two lines of thought into one. Duthie said that much of Preston Down had only recently been enclosed, with a road passing over it 'being the regular route for droves of sheep, from the western fairs, towards the metropolis and grazing districts of the south-eastern counties'. At Totford, he added, the 'thoroughfare [traffic] at certain times of the year was still very considerable, and a bridge had recently been built'.

He thought the road had been originally built by the Romans 'leading from their numerous stations in the north-western part of the country, towards their ancient station at Farnham' – a station that has since been discounted, with no reflection on Duthie's observation. 'North-western' looks puzzling in relation to the Lunways Inn, till the special map provided with the book is examined. It then emerges that as he saw it the road past the inn led only towards Alresford, thus preserving an east–west course for the Lunway, while the road to Totford and Preston Down was the one that used to come in from East Stratton.

Finally there is Isaac Taylor's large-scale map of 1759, not completely accurate but presenting a picture before turnpikes and enclosures had altered the whole appearance of the countryside. At the point east of the future A33, where the Lunway subsequently vanished, it came to open downland that extended across the line of the future turnpike. This was before the Lunways Inn was built to tempt it off course. It continued to drift as a separate route, rather north of Pile's Farm, now Burntwood House, and joined the complex of tracks around Itchen Wood that led to Abbotstone and the Itchen between Martyr Worthy and Itchen Stoke.

Perhaps the most plausible explanation of the Lunway is that it was an early attempt to find an easy passage of the rivers Test and Itchen, avoiding the heavy forests and steep hills that guarded Winchester. It would have Iron Age links with Old Sarum and Woolbury through to Oliver's Battery at Abbotstone, conforming to what seems to be a general principle of Iron Age throughways, that they shunned direct approach to the walled enclosures. As pastoral commerce grew, the Stockbridge and Itchen Stoke crossings would have created natural funnels, initially for local use. In due course they would link up, offering an east–west route of service to all other routes existing or to come, extendable or curtailed as the needs of different ages demanded. Seen in this light, the Lunway makes a logical passage between the two rivers. Little wonder, if the name can be so interpreted, that it was 'the popular downland route'.

Even today the Wessex downs are straddled with tracks, duplicating and criss-crossing each other, some made in this decade, some going back to remote times. Pre-Roman peoples were not the only ones to travel along the ridgeways and downlands. The early tracks may have gone out of use for centuries, to be revived again from the late 1600s when the growth of London made it profitable to drive cattle there from the West Country. What is a fact is that the course of many old routes was altered during the enclosure up-heavals of the eighteenth and early nineteenth centuries, and the Lunway may well have been among them. Here, prob-ably, is the origin of the tradition of a London way past the Lunways Inn and the Candover stream at Totford. But it is a tradition some 200 years old, not 2,000!

MICHELDEVER CROSSWAYS

The road system that must for centuries have centred on Micheldever is one of the most curious in Hampshire, be-cause it has become utterly lost. A glance at the map with its indicated streams and valleys will show that the place is on the obvious route from Stockbridge towards Alton and beyond, and this is how it would first have been known. Its later purpose would have been to link northern Wessex (towns like Newbury) with Winchester to the south, but this also became obscured. As a traffic centre Michel-dever began to decline in Stuart times, slipped further in Georgian days, and was finally killed in the present motor-ing age by a deliberate neglect of its road network.

The Georgian decline was brought about when the Basing-stoke–Winchester A33 road was constructed as a turnpike about 1758. Naturally the new road took the through traffic away from the old parallel but twisty way through Michel-dever, except for the canny ones like William Cobbett who hated paying tolls and continued to ride 'through the villages', as he termed it. By contrast with the leisurely meanderings of the village route, the new road followed the straight path of its Roman predecessor, and for coaches there was no change of horses between Winchester and the Wheatsheaf at Popham Lane.

Roughly halfway between the two stood the great mansion at East Stratton Park, and it was here that was struck the earliest blow at Micheldever. The chief family in the village in Elizabeth I's days were the same Wriothesleys who became Earls of Southampton and were better known at Titchfield. Deciding that the Micheldever house was below their status they set about building a more glamorous affair at nearby East Stratton. This is thought to have happened in the first half of the 1600s, and is supported by Norden's little-known manuscript map of Hampshire (1595) which carefully marks the residences of the nobility and gentry, but shows no house of consequence in East Stratton. This would mean that the place was built by the son of that Lord Southampton who was such an ardent backer of Shakespeare.

House-building on that scale meant a park, and in the usual manner part of East Stratton village was pulled down, to increase the empaled area, and re-erected slightly to the south. By 1664 licence had already been given to enclose the road from East to West Stratton and Overton, so that the line between the two sister villages was broken and a walk from one to the other meant circumventing the southern side of the park. What must have seemed the end of everything was the edict that the affairs of the parish, which hitherto had been conducted from Micheldever, should now be controlled from the new house in the outlying hamlet.

The credit for disclosing the earlier fame of Micheldever as a road centre must go to the unknown gentleman (and those who succeeded him) who in the opening years of the 1600s published the first Hampshire road mileage guide. Till then the Elizabethan county maps that had appeared were devoid of roads. To fill the gap until the roads were inserted these guides were issued, giving distances between the main posting towns and villages. In the case of Hampshire all the names seemed justified except that they included this neglected village of Micheldever. They made no mention of Popham Lane, which was destined in some degree to take its place.

BASINGSTOKE–MICHELDEVER–WINCHESTER

The history of this Micheldever locality has undoubtedly been belittled owing to the old Roman road from Winchester to Silchester which people have taken for granted as having functioned, regardless both of maintenance and of the Saxon settlements that developed a mile or two on either side of it, from the time when it was built until it formed the foundation on which the present road was laid. This attitude is reflected in the detailed and valuable *History of Micheldever* by the Rev A. B. Milner, which does not even refer to the making of the Georgian Turnpike that in fact was constructed for much of its length slightly west of the Roman foundations. This can be seen from a current Ordnance map (prior to the road widening) which shows the line of the Roman route inside the wall of Stratton Park; sufficient proof that the old highway was certainly not in use when the park boundry was fixed.

Important negative evidence regarding the earlier non-use of the Roman road is to be found (though he missed its significance) in Milner, who quoted various records relating to road maintenance in the area, not one of which concerned the Roman highway. On the contrary, he gives an inquisition of 1419 which showed that it had passed out of service even in that comparatively early period, and by the lack of reference to it may at that point have ceased to exist. The inquisition dealt with the failure by the then landlords, Hyde Abbey, to repair 'a certain highway of the Lord King lying in the ville of Micheldever by which goes from the ville of East Stratton as far as the ville of West Stratton,

in which the ford is ruinous . . .' This no doubt was the un-
fortunate road that, as has been seen, was to be closed
some 250 years later when the new house at East Stratton
was emparked.

The origin of the name Stratton is the Street of the Roman
road, with West Stratton on one side and East Stratton on
the other. The way between the two crossed the path of the
Roman road and at that time ran along by the little stream,
while the ford could easily have been a relic of the original
Roman crossing. Yet there is no mention of this Roman
way across the Stratton road. The only highway mentioned
– and that repeatedly – is the one between the two Strattons, whose land on both sides had belonged to the abbot;
his predecessors 'from time immemorial' had scoured and
repaired the ditch on its west side – probably the overgrown
ditch alongside the Roman way.

It is recorded that Edward I stayed for most of a fort-
night at nearby Woodmancott in the autumn of 1285 and
clearly found the road system adequate and more capaci-
ous than it is today. He visited Micheldever twice and once
went to Overton, a town of importance in the wool days
which had been expanded by the Winchester bishops early
in the 1200s, with the old village and church remaining north
of the Test as it still does, but the new market town south
of it on the way to Micheldever crossroads – a development
of Overton that has been repeated in the 1960s.

A hint of the local road system can even be traced back
to the Conquest. Evidence suggests that William I's march on
Winchester in 1066, after his victory at Hastings, took him
through Surrey to Farnham along the Harroway and onwards by its lower branch to Ellisfield and Farleigh Wallop, Nutley, Dummer and Micheldever.

These old records do not prove that the Roman road
was entirely out of commission in medieval days; in fact
the line of it, then called Longbank or Grimsdyke, was
clear to Stukeley when he was visiting Silchester in the
early 1700s, shortly before the turnpike was built. But they
do show that the ways in common use were those trodden

by post-Roman residents, and all in all it does look as though the Roman route between Popham Lane and Kings Worthy had not proved acceptable either to Saxons or Normans. Except for a fraction of Popham there was no village or major building anywhere along its length, and thus it becomes possible to see what manner of system, 'through the villages' as Cobbett said, proved more popular. The general line was developed rather west of the A33 road, though it must again be stressed that places like Woodmancott and Burghcote, which are now isolated, were in those days of more consequence and part of a well-linked network.

Taylor's 1759 map must give a fair impression of the earlier system after allowance is made for the changes at Stratton Park. But it must be noted that it was exactly contemporary with the Bill of 1758 establishing the new turnpike, and may be misleading in that the line was drawn on the map before the exact route of the road was surveyed; in other words, before it was built. Taylor may have used the rough line of the old Roman way, though, in fairness to him, he did not mark the road as 'turnpike' as was his normal practice, nor were there shown tollgates or milestones, either on this road or on the Basingstoke–Stockbridge road that branches off at Popham Lane and was approved as a turnpike in 1755.

The pre-turnpike traveller from Basingstoke to Winchester had two main choices, one taking him through Dummer, which until quite recently was connected with Preston Candover and Woodmancott. By the latter village he would have found his way, as did Edward I, to the Strattons and Micheldever. The alternative road to Winchester continued from Basingstoke to the Wheatsheaf Cross (as it would in time be termed) at Popham Lane and thus to the village of Popham, most of which has disappeared but lay west of the present road, although the modern signpost points east. It stood on a long bow of the road. Past the vanished New Inn it returned to the line of the A33 at the London Lodge entrance to Stratton Park. Here in pre-park days it had obviously continued to the original village of East Stratton and so to West Stratton, but when the park was made it had to rebound from London Lodge and make a direct cut to West Stratton.

Thence, though no road exists today, the highway continued across the stream to Micheldever, from which a series of parallel downland routes led to Kings or Headbourne Worthy. The present Hawthorn or Winchester Lane in Micheldever was one of them, though it did not need, as now, to connect with the A33, but kept a parallel route west of it, linking with what seemed to be the most used road, dignified as the Winchester highway. This is the road that runs by Weston, the suburb of Micheldever north of the stream, carrying this remarkable and most ancient highway across the downs to Overton and northward again to Kingsclere.

STOCKBRIDGE–MICHELDEVER–ALTON

Thus, then, from north to south of this busy junction at Micheldever, ran the roads to Winchester from Basingstoke and from Kingsclere or the Midlands. And with that rather complicated background disposed of, it is easier to see what was perhaps the prime function of the village, to act as a stopping-place between Stockbridge on the Test and the east – Alton and beyond. Once again, the throughway is no longer open.

A look at the present road westward from Micheldever to Sutton Scotney discloses a deep holloway, surrounded with all the evidence of pre-Roman occupation. Clearly it was in use in Saxon times, following the little nameless stream that finally joins the Test near Wherwell. In reverse, the course of stream and road from the Test is southwards through Barton Stacey and Bullingdon to Sutton Scotney, then eastwards by Wonston and Stoke Charity, and so to Micheldever. Thence the road continued eastwards along Dukes Lane (Ducks Lane they were once content to call it) and, till recently, journeyed to Brown Candover and Totford, with its links to

Alton and Alresford and Odiham. This is clearly the route, mentioned earlier in this chapter in connexion with the Lunway, that was known to Duthrie in the 1830s.

Sutton Scotney, the village where the nameless stream turns north, is the nearest to Stockbridge of the villages just listed. It would be natural from very early times for the eastern route from Stockbridge to proceed to Sutton Scotney, natural for it to continue along the stream to Micheldever, and thus equally natural for the first medieval route between Stockbridge and Basingstoke to follow this village-by-village way, on either side of the stream.

The more direct short cut over the downs from Sutton Scotney to Popham Lane would have come about as soon as the traffic warranted it, not impossibly with the offerings of facilities, hitherto only available at Micheldever, by some enterprising Boniface whose crossroads premises would later find fame as the Wheatsheaf, Popham Lane. The exact route, like many another, could become a source of friction between neighbouring parishes, both intent on avoiding its maintenance. It was only when the turnpike was made in the 1750s that the line was finally settled.

The road followed by Ogilby's surveyor in 1675 ran rather closer to Micheldever than it does nowadays. Although it approached Sutton Scotney, as at present, through 'Cranborne a small village', it was apparently in sight of Micheldever church. Ogilby was usually most careful in references of this nature, and he made a curious slip in showing the 'bourn' at Cranborne but omitting the larger stream at Sutton Scotney. It is not unlikely that his surveyor confused the two and was in reality taking a route far closer to the valley than he realized.

Even more striking evidence, relating to the same locality sixty years after Ogilby, comes from Milner's *History of Micheldever*. Read in conjunction with the uncertain Ogilby route, it provides a vivid illustration of the slow process by which the whole course of a road could be changed, with the offending parish cutting up or othwise obstructing the old highway, and throwing open a path to the new in the next parish.

Milner describes a case concerning this hamlet of Cranborne, well north of the stream, through which the present highway A30 runs, and its neighbour Hunton, a waterside hamlet on the north bank. He quotes a court roll of 1734 presenting 'the owners and occupiers of lands in Hunton for turning the King's Highway out of the tything of Hunton into the tything of Cranborne without any legal authority'. The quarrel continued at any rate till 1740, just prior to the Turnpike Bill, when the last recorded complaint was made to compel the inhabitants of Hunton to return the highway to where it anciently went through their own tything. As the event proved, they never did!

CHAPTER THREE

The Two Capitals

WINCHESTER TO LONDON

IN strict priority the Winchester road network should be the first to be discussed. Some of its western extensions have been dealt with earlier because the most important aspect of Winchester is the development of its connexions eastward with the Thames and London, and it seemed more helpful to clear some of the other ground in preparation. For between the Itchen in the Winchester area and the Thames in the Staines area there are traces of links that go back to an age which preceded the Roman occupation, and only one thing is certain, that the modern main roads that join the two are for the most part newcomers.

The Gough map of 1360 showed a route from Winchester to London that must have spread from Saxon village to Saxon village, probably with the impetus pushing northwards from the southern capital. Its later history is examined in Chapter 4; here it suffices to say that this Saxon line across Hampshire, through Alresford and Alton to Farnham, remained the principal route till the coming of the railways or, for that matter, the motor-car. From Farnham the line has not been so consistent, but in the Gough map it reached London via Guildford and Kingston, the one-time royal Saxon township.

As regards Hampshire, the line taken by the present A31 is mostly a turnpike construction of some 200 years ago, and it is essential to decide which of the various ways between Winchester and Alresford would have been regarded by the Saxons as the main road, if any particular way had that honour. As a start it is useful to motor over the fast dual carriageway between these two places, noting that the town on today's main road, New Alresford, was a new market speculation of about 1200, based on the original village of Old Alresford across the stream. The road, as was clear when it was a slower one a few years ago, crosses a ridge of downland which the much-travelled William Cobbett classed as 'amongst the most barren in England'. It offers no shelter, no villages, it is the reverse of direct, and it leaves Winchester by a mountainous ascent up St Giles Hill. Not the sort of road a Saxon farmer would have taken if he had an easier choice.

Yet there has long been a tendency – at any rate from the days of Sir George Rodney some 200 years ago – to regard this as the old and ancient way, though the only possible reason for such an opinion is that people have associated Winchester's communications with Roman roads, and when they found a straight road leading from the east gate they just insisted that it was the old Roman road like those from the other gates. But nobody yet has found a scrap of evidence that it was a Roman road, and from the look of old maps it was not as straight in the past as it is today.

Before the alternative routes offered by the Itchen valley are studied, it is necessary to note a couple of factors created by that wandering river and its tributaries. A major factor is the main-road water crossing, the Tichborne branch of the Itchen, just west of New Alresford, which is barely viewable under the parapet of the bridge. To complete the uprooting of nature's intentions, at the foot of the hill there is a railway bridge and embankment, the charming little railway being at this moment under threat of closure. Even so it is clear that the original lie of the land, influenced a few yards downstream by other converging tributaries, would have been excessively marshy.

The other factor is that a few hundred yards upstream there is a ford of drier access which connects with an old lane from Tichborne Down to Bishops Sutton that must certainly antedate New Alresford. It seems to have been a possibly pre-Roman route that came from the Twyford/

Owslebury direction, and a recent re-reading of a Saxon land charter of the 900s may be significant in describing the stretch of this lane along Tichborne Down past the Cricketers' Inn as 'the street'. The use of that term in those early days is often strong evidence of a route that had been straightened and strengthened in Roman times; the lane remains straight to this day.

In addition to this upstream ford, a short distance downstream from the main road is another crossing at Itchen Stoke which has certainly been in use since Saxon times. To have introduced a third ford between the two, in unsuitable ground, would have seemed superfluous, and the case against its ancient origin is supported by the fact that in Saxon days it was apparently nameless. Had they developed it, there would normally have been a hamlet on the site.

The earliest trace of a name for this A31 crossing so far found is as late as Ogilby's road survey of 1675, when it was marked 'small river called Sewers Water'. 'You go through Sewers Water, another branch of the Itchen so called,' he wrote. Sewer in medieval times meant an artificial watercourse for draining marshy land. It could also mean – with its alternate Seward – an official responsible for such work.

It so happens that this crossing of the Itchen appears on two of Ogilby's scroll maps, obviously drawn independently of each other, of which the first is the more important and probably earlier Map 51. The second, maybe later, Map 97 has 'Sewers Bridge' ('Crossing Sewers Bridge,' said the accompanying text), and there is a temptation to see behind its construction the contemporary influence of Charles II, who was so active in the neighbourhood at that time. A hundred years later 'Sewer' had changed to 'Seward', a name and spelling which it retains today, but which is not, as some would have it, the surname of an early benefactor.

Finally, in an endeavour to see the upper Itchen as the Saxons saw it, a subsequent Norman economic venture must be removed from the picture. At about the year 1200, the See of Winchester had fostered the development of various new or enlarged market towns, and New Alresford was one of them. It is generally recorded that, as part of this venture, the large Alresford Pond with its still extant Great Weir was constructed, so as to maintain a canal waterway on the Itchen and make it navigable from Southampton to Winchester and on to Alresford. Recent intensive local research has failed to find any documentary or physical evidence to support the whole of this tale. It could well be that the excessively marshy, but potentially rich agricultural land around the various streams was drained by a series of 'sewers', and that the pond was formed with its dam both to facilitate drainage and to act as a giant millpond to provide water power for the numerous new mills that the town required. There seems no reason why the Itchen should not in any case have been navigable for much of its length to Alresford. But beyond that, the one important point – and it is one which has dictated the course of the traffic ever since – was the decision to make the new town, New Alresford, on the opposite side of the stream to Old Alresford.

Prior to this event, the way from Winchester towards London would without question have led directly to Old Alresford, Bighton and Alton, the latter part of the route being in use as the main London road till the mid-1700s. This direct way across the Itchen was a mile or more shorter than the later one to New Alresford. The advantage of the New Alresford route was that, once the crossing at 'Sewers Water' (the Itchen extension towards Tichborne and Cheriton) had been drained and made passable, it offered a simpler, narrower ford across the river, with only one stream, against the several watercourses which beset the Old Alresford route. Moreover, for traffic to and from Southampton it provided a saving of several miles across the downs to Twyford by avoiding Winchester altogether.

Meanwhile, it is the situation before the arrival of Norman New Alresford which has to be considered; the way taken, from the moment he left Winchester, by a traveller to London who would be aiming towards Old Alresford and Bighton beyond it. When these two last sites were established in Saxon times there was no great man-made pond to influence their positioning; just the little Alre stream running down to meet the Itchen and the Candover, with a wide area of marsh above Itchen Stoke.

A modern map, with its complex of trackways north of the river, shows how many of them interweave and converge near Abbotstone (Illus. 6), which with its big house was once a place of considerably more moment than it is at present. The house, in its last days owned by a Duke of Bolton, continued in use till the 1700s when the village with its church had all but vanished. One reason for its desertion may have been the decline of the thoroughfare now under discussion. Even on a small-scale map it can be seen how the tracks from the valley road between Martyr Worthy and Itchen Stoke bend towards Abbotstone, and a visit to this forgotten traffic centre will disclose traces of other tracks running south of Abbotstone across the little Candover stream, on to Alresford. The ground evidence is still so strong that, even without the written support quoted at the end of this section, there can be no doubt that the early line of the Saxon-Norman road to London ran through Abbotstone to Old Alresford, both of which places were named in the Domesday survey.

But if the choice of Abbotstone was dictated by simple issues of geography, the route between Abbotstone and Winchester presents a very different problem, with at least three alternatives. The obvious road, since it involves no crossing of the Itchen, is that from the north gate of the city to Kings Worthy, then bending with the river to the existing track which leaves B3047 between Martyr Worthy and Itchen Abbas, and, till recently, led direct to Abbotstone. The missing stretch from a point just south of Itchen Down Farm is shown on maps of last century.

This route would have duplicated the Saxon procedure from the south gate of Winchester, using the existing Roman hardway as an exit from the city, and then breaking away from it so as to follow the river bank. The continued im-

portance of this Roman stretch is shown by the building by
it of the new Hyde Abbey; the 1100s saw the construction
of three great establishments in the Winchester suburbs,
Hyde on the northern exit, St Cross on the southern and St
Mary Magdalene on the eastern way over St Giles Hill.

The second choice of a route lay from the east gate (or
north-east Durngate) to Easton and then, by the ford at
Chilland, to the track by Itchen Down Farm just mentioned. From Winchester the way led through Winnall, an
area notorious for flooding, though the sunken Easton Lane
bears witness both to its antiquity and its past volume of
traffic. This route, at any rate in dry weather, would be
preferred to the first, being shorter and more direct from
within the city. But the third route, although much of it
has vanished, may have been the general choice in spite of
its initial drawback of the steep climb up St Giles Hill. It
was just as short and probably more practicable in bad
weather. Its likely origin deserves careful study.

As the Saxon homesteads were established along the
upper Itchen, the names along the south bank would have
spread from Easton to Avington, Yavington, Lovington
and Ovington. The middle two are still retained as house-
names. The waterside road would have linked these hamlets
and followed the bends of the river to Tichborne and Cheriton. A more direct road eastwards would have been the next
stage from Winchester, up St Giles Hill and over the downs
to join the riverside way at Tichborne and Cheriton. It was,
in fact, the first essay at the modern A272 Winchester–
Petersfield road. It was in use till the early 1700s, passing
south of Tichborne and reaching Cheriton along a lane
which can still be found just above the church marked 'No
through road'. The middle part of the route has long since
been ploughed up. Mud was the main trouble. There were at
least two more eighteenth-century attempts starting from the
lane opposite Avington Lodge on the A31, which must represent the original line of the road over Magdalen Down.
They ran south of Cheriton, had appalling reputations as
bad roads, and never became turnpikes. The present A272,

with its separate approach to Winchester over Cheesefoot
Hill, was an old track made into a turnpike as late as 1825
(Illus. 8).

But the road up St Giles Hill evidently came to mean
something far more important. It was found, as the need
grew to strengthen communications north-eastwards towards London, that it provided a valuable all-weather,
marsh-avoiding route to a river crossing by Itchen Abbas,
and thus by the Abbotstone road to Old Alresford, Alton
and beyond. Its method of leaving Winchester is significant.
It took the east gate road up St Giles Hill for a matter
of two miles. Just by the milepost, on today's A31, is a
small turning to the north marked 'Easton' by Magdalen
Hill Farm. A glance into the field on the left of the lane will
show a mound of grass, the remains of the Hospital of St
Mary Magdalene which gave its name to the hill that in the
fulness of time, when the hospital was forgotten, became
Morning or, as known today, Morn Hill.

Reference has already been made to the two other great
Norman establishments – Hyde and St Cross – on the north
and south Roman roads outside the walls of Winchester.
What is remarkable about this third site, the hospital on the
east road, can be seen in the Ordnance Survey map of Roman Britain, where the first two miles up St Giles Hill are
marked 'Roman road, course uncertain'. It is noticeable
how often the Normans, when selecting a site for some
monastic or military building, related it to a Roman hardway which must have been in active use. In the present instance the Romans, once they had provided a firm road up
St Giles Hill and out of the city, may have had no need to
continue it as a made-up one, since it would only have
been a minor route avoiding the forests east of the Alre and
Wey streams.

The old hospital, established in the 1100s, became in time
a sort of almshouse, was knocked about by Dutch prisoners
in the wars of the late 1600s, was never properly repaired
and was finally demolished in the late 1700s. Its significance
to the present purpose is its siting, which appears meaning-

less until it can be seen as its founders saw it, an institution comparable with St Cross on the Southampton road. For though there is now no sign of it at all, the field on the left was once cut by a diagonal road, a major route from Winchester to Alton. It forked down towards Avington on the waterside through a line of ancient earthworks past the derelict Mud Farm, which is shown on modern maps Mud Farm is a kind of romantic ghost; its situation corresponds with a large but unnamed house on Norden's manuscript map of Hampshire of the 1590s; the ploughed earth that surrounds it is full of broken pottery.

The reputation of this road was such that up to the mid-1700s, when it died, or rather was put to death, it was still called the Alton road, long after the main Alton road had been routed through New Alresford. It had an extension towards Southampton, round the back of St Giles, that bypassed Winchester and emerged by the other hospital at St Cross. The map will show how much shorter is a line from the top of St Giles Hill to New Alresford, let alone the older route to Old Alresford, than is the roundabout A31 pursued today. What killed the old road was the decision to take the new (1756) turnpike London road along its present A31 course, which roughly corresponds with the original road to Petersfield with a left turn to New Alresford. A tollgate (Short Sledge by name) was placed just clear of the city at the top of St Giles Hill and shortly before the traveller reached the old Alton road. He had to pay for the turnpike whether he liked it or nor. Maps show that the old road and the old hospital were both there till about 1790. By 1800 they had vanished.

Yet another factor must be remembered in connexion with the absolute maze of tracks that wander so rampantly on maps of Magdalen Hill when it was still open downland. St Giles Fair had been established in Norman times, and it grew and grew. Everybody from all over the south and west and beyond went to it; eventually it lasted for weeks. In addition the Magdalene Hospital was granted a fair, farther along the road. One of the problems in sorting out the roads around Winchester is the confusion caused by the fair-ground tracks, all centred on the top of St Giles Hill.

Finally, the reason why the 1756 turnpike went along the top of Magdalen Down, the roundabout way, to New Alresford, also provides a simple explanation for its unnatural sharp left turn at the halfway mark. It has been shown how the early Petersfield road from Winchester continued beyond that turn. What really happened there was a cross-roads, in pre-turnpike days slightly south of the present turn, of which the Winchester end and the New Alresford end are the survivors, linked together, of two separate roads. The New Alresford end originally proceeded south to Twyford. It was in fact the main road from London to Southampton, the first Winchester bypass.

A copy of the original Turnpike Bill for this stretch of road, search for which has so far been unproductive, might throw light on the reason why it did not make a shorter diagonal cut from Magdalen Hill to Sewards Bridge near Alresford. The case for retaining the old route may have been that it could share toll receipts with traffic from the Petersfield road; that it would avoid an awkward, well-wooded terrain; that the alternative route would have been opposed by the Buckingham family at Avington, who were expanding their parkland.

In this complex hubway of English history, the upper Itchen, what sort of picture has so far emerged? The present main road A31 is comparatively modern, made some 200 years ago through Farnham to Alton, Chawton and New Alresford, as part of the London–Southampton and London–Poole turnpike roads. Prior to that the London–Southampton road had for many centuries bypassed Winchester, running direct from New Alresford to Morestead and Twyford. Before that again was a road system, centred on the capital, Winchester, which the early Normans used when they took over from the Saxons. This system was generous. It embraced a wide network of trackways which had been developed by earlier inhabitants, following the tops of the downs from east to west, sometimes in parallel lower down the slope, with numerous north–south intersections between each ridge of down. Many of these trackways are still in use.

In addition there were such stretches of hard Roman road as the Saxons had found it worthwhile to incorporate into their own system, and many more stretches which were neglected. Eventually had come the Saxons' own contribution, at source a linking-up of their village settlements along the Itchen, but extending, as the kingdom extended its communications towards the Thames, so that it surmounted the hilltop which separated it from the Wey at Alton.

Their route towards London from Winchester must have been taken through Abbotstone and Old Alresford, and, of the various ways of reaching Abbotstone, there are grounds for believing that the most popular would have been one that remained in use till some 200 or less years ago, known in the 1600s as the Alton road. (The A31 road from Winchester is still called the Alresford road on the city map; there is no London road.) It ran up St Giles Hill for two miles, then forked left towards the river at the spot where the Normans later sited their Magdalene Hospital. It passed by Mud Farm to Avington village, through mid-Georgian extensions at Avington which affected not only the park but the river itself have destroyed most of its traces hereabouts. Its apparent course has been noted in a sunken way in the wood west of Pits Farm, and at one time it may have passed close by Avington Park, a house of ancient foundations. Contemporary maps suggest that it reached the Itchen at the end of the park palings east of the present Itchen Abbas bridges and close to where the sawmills used to be. There are still footbridges at that point which coincide with the parish boundaries. An old Avington Park estate map shows a ford, and the existing line of trees marking an early approach way to the house seems to have borne the name of 'the old London road'. Across the river it connected with an existing – and otherwise apparently purposeless – trackway leading direct to Abbotstone.

Once the line of this route is appreciated, it makes sense

of several documentary clues which were previously without meaning. As far back as the reign of William I, for example, there is an old and oft-repeated tradition which, whether true or not, must have had a practical interpretation to those who heard it. William had given permission for as much timber as could be cut in a day from his Hampnage Wood to be donated to the building of the new Winchester cathedral. The bishop got busy with everybody he could muster, and the king was appalled, on his next journey from London, to see that the whole wood had been cut down. But only by riding through Avington on the route described could William have sighted what had happened. Another famous but even earlier tradition is associated with Hampnage Wood, that of the one tree which was spared, the Saxon Gospel Oak, again with its easiest access from the line of this road.

Next, in 1101, Duke Robert, eldest son of William the Conqueror, when claiming the throne had moved his invading force from Portsmouth Harbour towards Winchester. Hearing that Queen Matilda was lying there in childbirth, he politely avoided the city and decided to march to London instead. It is recorded (perhaps the first known written reference to the road) that he took the London road by Alresford to Alton. It can easily be seen that for an army to march towards Alton through (Old) Alresford from the Winchester direction, it must have followed a route such as this.

Leland was in New Alresford about 1540 and did not leave it by the A31 road. He departed by 'end of the town' with its bridge and made his way, presumably through Abbotstone, to the riverside by Itchen Stoke to Kings Worthy, noting wood bridges at Stoke and Easton. His mileage figures were too erratic to assist location. Later he noted that 'eastward of Winchester on the top of (St Giles) Hill was the way to London' which led through Alresford at a distance of seven miles; information that proves nothing.

Celia Fiennes, recording her horseback journeys around 1698, described the route exactly. She was proceeding from

Farnham (Surrey) to Winchester; she passed the Duke of Bolton's house at Abbotstone, on the side of a hill with fine gardens and much fruit; she went along on the hills in sight of the river 'All' – it was a good chalky way; then there was the hospital on 'Maudline Hill', a large rambling building like a little town; finally the fairground, noted for its hops and cheese and a vast array of 'Waines' (wagons) especially from the West Country. Miss Fiennes' reference to the major stream, now called the Itchen, by the name of its tributary the 'All' (Alre) is common. As recently as the nineteenth century it seems to have been regularly described as the Alre, not the Itchen, as far as and even below Winchester.

Not long after came Daniel Defoe, who took a similar route. From New Alresford he passed the Duke of Bolton's house at Abbotstone, adding 'from hence, at the end of seven miles over the downs, we came to Winchester'.

A DIRECT WAY TO FARNHAM

In assessing the various road systems that have joined Winchester with Farnham and London, it has been seen that the present route from Winchester, the A31, has no antiquarian significance and indeed is unlikely to have existed before the founding of New Alresford about 1200. The Saxon and Norman ways can only have led through Abbotstone. What then of the enigma that has puzzled historians for centuries, whether there was a Roman road east or north-east of Winchester and, if so, where? A serious modern school of study remains convinced that a road led in Roman times from the city towards Farnham and the Hog's Back. Indeed, the ground evidence of Roman buildings is so intense in the valleys of the upper Itchen and the Wey that some form of reasonable communication must be accepted as a fact, even if unlocated.

But a reasonable form of communication need not imply a hard-core road all the full distance. The Solent area was amply provided with a defensive network of hard roads,

to Chichester from London and Silchester, to Porchester
from Chichester and Southampton and Winchester, to Winchester from Silchester and Southampton. Within that gran-
diose framework the more domestic roads would not have
needed such solid treatment except where conditions warranted it. Many of them would have been based on the lay-
out of tracks that the Romans found when they entered the
country, and which the native population would have continued to use.

Certainly experienced antiquarians of the seventeenth and
eighteenth centuries – Aubrey, Camden, Stukeley – claimed
to have noticed Roman sections in the road between Winchester and Farnham. The non-antiquarian Defoe said the
same thing. But in only one case is there a clue to the exact
road they took, and it is not impossible for road repairs,
such as are known to have been actively carried out
between Alresford Pond and Medstead on the then main
road, to have been mistaken for Roman work. The
traveller who did leave a clue to his route was Defoe. Referring to the local belief in a great Roman highway to London he wrote, not long after 1700, 'we nowhere see any
remains of it, except between Winchester and Alton, and
chiefly between Alresford and Alton'. As has been said,
his road between Winchester and Alresford was that which
branched off from the top of Magdalen Down by the old
hospital, the two-mile stretch from the city that is shown on
the Ordnance Survey map as of Roman origin.

It is quite feasible to estimate the line between Winchester and Farnham in days before the Saxons developed
their particular form of valley route. In Roman or pre-
Roman times it would certainly have been more direct and
would have gained the advantage of a higher level. It is most
easily seen in reverse, to Winchester or the immediate
downland from the hill above Farnham by the castle, for its
line thereabouts can be settled without hesitation. The
course of the Harroway is a pre-Roman route accepted by
the Ordnance Survey as being used in that area by the Romans, and its more southerly leg kept along the ridge to a

point on the outskirts of Alton where it turned westward away from Winchester. This point has always been a road junction, and even the inn that stands near it carries the tradition of a Roman hoard in its name, the Golden Pot. This curious name, which others have associated with a Roman signpost, might be merely a romantic version of an Old or Olden Post, an early guidepost which perhaps preceded the inn.

From the Golden Pot the most likely line would be south of Shalden, which has provided Roman relics, and across the valley where an old path runs to the bridle track at Thedden that leads through Wivelrod to the pre-Roman encampment on the hilltop at Medstead. A thirteenth-century document, donating land at Thedden to Selborne Priory, refers to a boundary as the 'Stony Strat' which can only mean a made-up road, perhaps a hardening of the way down the steep stretch of hillside. There is written evidence of a highway from the Medstead encampment through Hattingley and Heath Green, where it is clear enough that the road continued towards Godsfield south of Wield, passing a tumulus and the site of a Roman villa. Godsfield, remote enough now, still possesses the remains of a Norman chapel connected with the Knights Hospitallers who were especially associated with work on behalf of travellers or pilgrims; a site they selected would normally be on a busy thoroughfare.

The road passed by the Iron Age enclosure at Oliver's Battery and so to Abbotstone. Here it would have continued by any of the three ways already described, by Magdalen Hill, by the ford at Chilland (again with Roman connexions) to Easton and Winnall, or to the north gate of Winchester by joining the Roman hard road from Silchester at Kings Worthy.

It may be added that the main evidence from the Iron Age on this route, continuing from the Winchester area to Oliver's Battery, Medstead, Holybourne Down along the Harroway, tends to link it, not with Farnham, but with Caesar's Camp just north of it. The connexion would have

been by the Maulthway track which left the Harroway
south of Crondall and has been traced across the Aldershot heathland to a crossing of the Blackwater stream at
Coleford in Farnborough, near the Mytchett, and so to
Chobham Ridges.

A DIRECT WAY TO THE THAMES

Finally, in this consideration of Winchester's communications with the north-east when its prestige was at its highest,
comes the evidence, well-supported even now, of a direct
route between the city and the Thames which would have
offered a saving of very many miles to earlier travellers.
Such a route, as a ruler will quickly show, must lead
through or near Odiham in north Hampshire; the need for
it is almost sufficiently established by the fact that nearby,
at North Warnborough, stood the royal Norman castle, halfway between London – or Windsor – and Winchester, but
isolated from any known road. It must have been the way
along which King John rode when he left Odiham for
Runnymede and Magna Carta in June 1215. He used it
considerably, as his itineraries show: January 1214, Staines–
Odiham–Winchester;   May   1215,   Winchester–Odiham;
June 1215, Winchester–Odiham, Odiham–Winchester.

A study of old maps, with present paths and lanes and
boundaries, can bring the road to life again. What happened
to it is clear enough. Its overriding purpose disappeared
with the decline of the castle; the need for contact between
the wool centres of Winchester and Odiham declined with
the wool trade; local needs took people round by the villages
while long-distance needs favoured a main road through
the population centres; the main road became focused on
Southampton and offered a saving in mileage; Winchester
was no longer a magnet justifying its own main road.
When Milne produced his large-scale map of Hampshire
in 1791 the traces were getting thin, though it was still possible to make a much straighter journey than can be made
today. It must surely have been the basis of an unfulfilled

plan about that time to create a new London turnpike road via Old Alresford and Odiham.

Like all the north-easterly ways from the Itchen valley, it ran through Abbotstone. Instead of branching off to Old Alresford and Alton as the main Saxon road did, it continued along the high-level route that, as just discussed, led to the heights above Farnham. Thus the two routes continue together past the old enclosure called Oliver's Battery, a not uncommon form of name around Winchester, which became closely involved in the affairs of the Civil War. In this case, applied to the Iron Age settlement, it has been derided, though it can now be seen as reasonable and a likely choice as a gun site to cover not only the Candover road that would lead to the great royalist headquarters at Old Basing, but equally the key road junction at Abbotstone. All the roads hereabouts are still visible, and in fact an old map suggests that the big house at Abbotstone had its main entrance avenue facing north to Oliver's Battery.

The road continued to the site of the Norman Godsfield chapel where there was a further fork, with the Farnham way branching right and the Odiham way continuing towards Wield Wood, where excavation of an earthwork at Barton Copse (1968) has produced evidence of another Norman building, possibly a fortified hunting-lodge. The road proceeded to Bagmore near Lasham, and Herriard.

In Bradley wood it was covered by an old fort called Hurst Castle, considered to be Norman. Near Herriard there was a crossroads with the Basingstoke–Alton road given in Ogilby's 1675 survey which was able, even at that late date, to show the directions to Winchester and Odiham. The modern Basingstoke–Alton road, A339, takes a different line from the earlier one, but the side road from it, through Weston Corbett to Upton Grey, must represent the passage of the Odiham route along the little Whitewater stream to the Norman castle at North Warnborough. The one-time dominance of the castle over its neighbouring town of Odiham can still be noted since its westward end, which should be the important road to Winchester, declines from its magnificent main street to a small lane that has to wander round to the outskirts of the castle.

As to the origin of such a route there is no genuine evidence. It is on a straightish line from the Norman Magdalene Hospital outside Winchester, and the examples of Norman buildings which have been quoted suggest that it was there before their arrival. In no sense is it a typical Saxon valley road and it is not specially related to the sites of Saxon villages. The whole of the district so far traversed by it is thick with traces of Roman, Roman-British and earlier dwellings, with which its general line is in sympathy. At Bagmore it meets a 'Coldharbour' which in the Hampshire countryside has never failed to denote a road known in Roman-British times. Immediately beyond the Norman castle site at North Warnborough the line meets yet another Roman villa.

At this point the Basingstoke Canal, built in the late 1700s, has caused a diversion of traffic through Odiham. It is easy to see that before its construction the way continued on across the common to Winchfield, almost certainly along the line past the church. Just north of the church stood the old manor house (Court Farm) which was owned by Chertsey Abbey, as was the neighbouring parish of Elvetham and the nunnery at Hartley Wintney. There must have been a well-used road between the Thames-side landlords and these Hampshire villages, at any rate until the Reformation.

Hereabouts also the early road from Basingstoke towards London could have joined this more direct course from Winchester, which proceeded by the outskirts of Elvetham, near what was once called 'Street End', a term that often denotes a road of antiquity. It approached the north side of Fleet Pond past another 'Coldharbour' (shown on Taylor's map of the mid-1700s) which appears to have been on the Forestry Commission land by the railway line adjoining the North Hants Golf Club. It is known that a medieval duty of Fleet Pond was to supply fish to Winchester for the bishop's table. Such an arrangement would have been laughable without the means of swift direct transport such as this road alone could have provided. Its use as a Norman trade route is also shown by the record that King John's cellars at North Warnborough Castle were supplied with wine from Staines.

The road continued towards Cove and the Blackwater stream on the borders of Frimley and Farnborough. Its passage took it close to two more 'Coldharbours', at a small wood in Yateley parish, and east of North Farnborough. Thus the way has met four 'coldharbours', the only ones out of fourteen inland Hampshire recordings which have not as yet been associated closely with the line of a road known to the Romans.

From here onwards the ground evidence, which has been abundant, becomes thin. Military and urban developments have disposed of it. Nevertheless, to pursue its course, or as near as can be got to it, is still a rewarding enterprise, taking in, for example, the Tudor buildings at Bramshot near Cove with the old 'Trunk Road' passing 'Trunk Farm'. The most probable site for crossing the Blackwater stream would be at Coleford Bridge where it would have met the road, mentioned earlier in this chapter, that came round from the Harroway.

It is here, with the entrance into Surrey, that a close study of Rocque's magnificent map of 1762, together with its overlapping fellow of Berkshire (1752), offers such compensation for the destruction on the ground. And since one of its most unexpected disclosures – and one that influences the whole picture – is to be found by the Thames at Staines, it will be easier to survey this Surrey portion from the Thames to the Blackwater rather than in the reverse direction which has been the plan so far.

From these maps of the mid-1700s it looks clear enough that on both sides of the Thames ran the typical Saxon river roads with the villages spaced along them. On the Surrey side the road ran from Old Windsor downstream past Staines (or Hythe) to Chertsey, where it is known today as the Windsor road. Away from the river settlements ran an inland road more or less parallel to the Thames on which stood places like Thorpe and Egham and Englefield.

What was to become the Great West road running from Staines Bridge inland and away from the Thames, through Egham to Bagshot, was perhaps a post-Saxon addition after the Norman causeway was built along the waterside. It does seem strange that this route should have been chosen, proceeding up the steep Egham Hill, when it could equally have made its objective with perhaps slightly less mileage by taking a course through Thorpe that would have avoided the hill altogether. Ogilby, usually so careful in these matters, made no mention of Egham Hill in his 1675 survey, but where its top would be he showed a straight continuation of the road (so often an indication of its original line) marked 'to Bagshot a different way', though there is no subsequent marking as to where it emerged. This must be the way that still appears on the maps as going to Egham Wick or Wick Heath, but by the 1700s it seems to have been lost, as now, in the intricacies of Windsor Park.

Students of Roman roads soon became aware that the famous route from London to Silchester is largely followed to this day by the highway through Middlesex till it reaches the Thames at Staines. Across the Thames its Surrey course is lost for some miles till it can be found again not far from Bagshot. This is what Codrington wrote in his classic *Roman Roads in Britain* of 1903:

The line crosses the Thames to Hythe a little to the south of the present bridge, and near the site of the old bridge, to the west of which Stukeley [mid-1700s] saw the old road very evidently go through the fields, the ridge being then visible; but no sign of it now appears. He traced it along a lane and a footpath towards Thorpe Lea … A stone pillar erected near Great Fosters in 1850 records that it marks the site of a Roman road, a portion of which remains in the adjoining meadow.

If this was so, concluded Codrington, this latter cannot have been a road to Silchester, but a branch road.

Now Stukeley the antiquary and Rocque the cartographer were for all practical purposes contemporaries, and what Stukeley described should be borne out by Rocque. And so it is. The map showed the old Staines bridge crossing the Thames to Hythe, just where those charming old houses and the riverside inn still by a miracle survive, bordering the old road to Chertsey. A short distance to the west, towards the present Staines bridge, a footpath struck inland, exactly parallel to the line of the old bridge, at right angles to the river. Here in the 1700s was a great open space called 'Hythe Field', running upstream as far as Egham village. At the time of Rocque's Surrey map the field had just become enclosed, though up to the present time small areas of open ground still represent it. A double check is provided by Rocque's map of Berkshire some ten years earlier in 1752. A generous overlap covered all this region of Surrey, though it was obviously a different drawing. The enclosure of Hythe Field in this map had only just started, while in the Surrey map it was almost all split up into small fields. The footpath appeared on both maps.

Beyond Hythe Field the straight line of the footpath continued on both maps into a hedged lane running to Thorpe Lea. Here its course was lost, as the lane turned northwards in a curious bend marked 'Pipe House', running along by the small stream there. But none of this straight stretch from the Thames – and whether Roman or not it must without question have been the stretch described by Stukeley as Roman – was proceeding in the direction required by the seekers of the Silchester road; this, on their contention, should have been sighted on Bakeham House and the big Egham Hill on which now stands the Royal Holloway College. (There has been a suggestion of a Roman foundation hereabouts, but it seems flimsy.) Rocque's Surrey map agreed with today's Ordnance Survey in showing the Middlesex line of the Roman road as reaching Bakeham House were it to be extended across the Thames. Such a

line, if extended to the top of Egham Hill, could run along
Ogilby's road to 'Bagshot a different way', the lane to Egham
Wick that gets lost in Windsor Park.

The alternative for the Silchester road would have been
to avoid Egham Hill by continuing from the Thames on a
line such as Stukeley's and then turning towards Bagshot
from the neighbourhood of Great Fosters, where the further
trace of a Roman road was located, apparently in extension from Stukeley's path. His evidence is so substantiated,
and is perhaps so seldom re-read, that it should be quoted
in full. It must be understood that in 1723, when he was in
Staines to trace the Roman route in the Antonine itinerary
that ran London–Calleva–Winchester, he thought that
'Calleva Atrebates', now recognized as Silchester, was
Farnham in Surrey, and the need for a Staines–Silchester-
road did not arise. The Farnham area, with Alice Holt
Forest, was nevertheless the centre of a lively Roman-
British pottery industry that would have needed a wide net-
work of minor trade routes. Stukeley wrote:

From Farnham the [Roman] road divides into two
branches with an acute angle: one goes to Guildford and
Darking, where it meets the Stane-street coming from
Chichester; the other to Stanes, which I prosecuted to
Farnborow, probably a station or inn, or camp to secure the road over this wild country: for it is deep sand
from Farnham to Egham: but where in particular the Roman road went is not easy to define, because of the extraordinary sandiness of the whole country: but at Frimley,
near here, about sixteen year ago, an urn with Roman
coins and intaglias was found. Mr Titchburn had them.
This is directly in the way to Farnborow ...

... Between Oxford-street and Stanes, this Roman
road was originally drawn through Brentford, which undoubtedly was a mansion then: and this is a very strait
line: I rode the broken part of it between Acton road and
Turnham Green: it is still a narrow strait way, keeping
its original direction, but full of dangerous sloughs, being

a clayey soil and never repaired: it butts full upon Stanes bridge, and then beyond it passes forward in a strait line through gardens and yards into the corn-fields, where its ridge is still left, the highest part of all the field, though they plough close to it on both sides; and it is now a road for three quarters of a mile; then it enters a narrow lane, and at last degenerates into a footpath toward Thorp–lea, in the way to Farnham: the common road leaving it all this way while in the way to Egham. So that undoubtedly Stanes was the Pontes of Antoninus; the distance of 22 miles on both sides answering the fact.

For good measure Stukeley added a sketch (Ilus. 15), taken from the river bank towards Egham, with the wide stretch of the 'common road' (the Great West or Land's End road) and in the background the massive piles of the old wooden bridge, with the gaps on either side of the middle to allow the passage of craft. What appears to have been the tollhouse for road and river traffic stood on the Surrey side. And then, in the sketch which he drew on 16th September, 1723, Stukeley had his road marked 'Calleva Atrebatum' proceeding inland and straightening out after its first curved way through Hythe Field which, in complete agreement with the two slightly later maps that have been described, was only just becoming enclosed, the enclosures starting from either side of the Roman way. No doubt it suffered the same fate as near Old Sarum, where he found 'the countrymen have attacked it vigorously on both sides with their ploughs: we caught them at the sacrilegious work, and reprehended them for it.'

The modern map shows a road that leads inland from the roundabout at Staines bridge and comes after half a mile to a distinct right bend, which after another half-mile makes on the right a wide inverted U-turn. This last part does seem to represent the Rocque map with its curious bend marked Pipe House, that has been mentioned. The stream is a useful check. These two maps, of Surrey and Berkshire, are not as accurate as modern standards require. They are not even aligned on the same north compass bearing – a fact which supports their independence of each other, especially as much of what they show is traceable today. The line of the road from Hythe probably represents the way that was followed by the Saxons to Windlesham and Bagshot before the route over Egham Hill was chosen. On the Berkshire map, the line circumvented the enclosures, still with us, of Milton Park and Great Fosters, and ran through to Stroud Green east of Callowhill, or Gallow Hill as Rocque knew it, adjoining Hangman's Hill. Here the enclosed farming area ended and the line continued over what is now the Wentworth Gold Course, formerly Potney Warren, though the network of lanes and dwellings kept to the cultivated land to the south, avoiding the open heath. On the line from Great Fosters there were at least three disconnected straight stretches of apparently purposeless road, aiming across the heath at King's Hill, north of Windlesham, and thus across the main A30 road east of Bagshot, where it is known that the Roman Silchester road changed course.

The Surrey map showed a similar picture through Stroud Green but was more concerned to give the situation throughout the country rather than towards the Berkshire border. Thus, from Stroud Green there was a southerly route that might have led off from the main Roman Silchester road. What did prove so astonishing was to find that it was immediately taking the line of some road of antiquity which was clearly identified by a succession of barrows. Much of it has now vanished, but it can be roughly traced on the 1-inch Ordnance map through Stroud, Trumps Green (near where the M3 motorway is scheduled to bisect it), across the common to its junction with the A320 east of Staple Hill, and south of Fox Hill partly along the line of the B386. Near Fox Hill there is a boundary record, perhaps Saxon, of a 'Ridge Street'.

The road continued south of Windlesham and Curley Hill to the point between White and Redroad hills where there is a junction with the Maulthway along Chobham

Ridges. The Maulthway here is a road name still in use, along the residential Camberley outskirts to the Jolly Farmer on the main A30 road. It is not impossible that the name was 'adopted' by this stretch when the original road at right angles went out of use. This would have been the Maulthway already noted as coming from Crondall beyond Farnham, of which the continuance towards Staines beyond the crossroads at Chobham Ridges has long since vanished.

The road ran westwards rather as it does today, dropping down the hill towards Frimley but keeping south of Tomlin's Pond towards the Surrey/Hampshire border at Frimley Green/Farnborough Street. Coleford bridge, near Mytchett, seemed to be an important crossing-point of the River Blackwater, but it is hard to get the exact spot since, apart from disturbances by the Basingstoke Canal and the railway, the river valley there seems to have been farmed in small units, and the old ways diverted, at a very early stage.

Whatever its origin, the course of this road or roads can be seen in sectors. There was a high-level way from the Thames at Staines to the Harroway near Farnham, apparently pre-Roman and perhaps used and strengthened during the occupation. Near Farnborough on the Hampshire border it joined another way that ran near Odiham to the Itchen valley by Winchester. In all that forty-five-mile stretch it seldom touched the centre of a village.

Winchester receded, and Odiham, the halfway point, receded. Farnham grew as a great corn and hop market, and in turn receded. The need for long-distance trade between such points and London vanished. But the roads remained – as roads always do – diverted in parts, lost in parts, performing a different function. It would not be surprising to learn that much of them was in use till the early part of the last century as cattle or similar droves.

CHAPTER FOUR

The London–Southampton Road

THE 'CENTRE' MOVES TO LONDON

IN its Saxon and early Norman development, the natural passage for communication between London and Southampton would have been through the capital city of Winchester, where it would have joined the Land's End road. Between the twin capitals of Winchester and London, the route followed the Saxon valley line through Old Alresford, Farnham and Guildford, and thus travellers from Southampton were taken several miles out of their road by visiting Winchester instead of making directly for Alresford over the downs from Twyford on the lower part of the River Itchen.

In the motoring 1900s the recognized main road from London to Southampton runs through Staines and Basingstoke and finds Winchester on its direct passage, a city that must be artificially bypassed. But until this present century, and despite the new routes that came about with the turnpike coaching era, the road through Basingstoke was never give pride of place, which remained with that through Farnham and Alresford. And for many centuries, from the decline of Winchester in medieval times till its revival in Georgian times, the old capital was deliberately bypassed by the short cut from Alresford towards Southampton.

When this cut was first brought into general use will be discussed shortly; it is unlikely to have been developed on a big scale until the creation of New Alresford about the year 1200. The Gough map, which has already been described as indicating the main roads of England in the mid-1300s, shows that the Land's End road at this period was

still recognized as proceeding from Farnham to Winchester
and Salisbury, but does not give the link to Southampton.
Its earliest mention seems to be in Grafton's *A Little
Treatise*, 1571. In Ogilby's great survey of 1675 the short
cut was officially recorded as the main road (Illus. 1).

With all these ways there would always have been alternative routes open to the knowledgeable. Guides were
being employed up to the outset of Victorian times, and
remarkably unreliable some of them proved to be, as Cobbett among others lamented. But adherence to the recognized main roads would have been the traveller's main hope
for lodging, stabling and the various crafts and trades demanded by horse transport. For the well-to-do and well
connected, with friends or relatives en route to offer hospi-
tality, the path was comparatively easy throughout the many
and varying centuries of horse travel. For the remainder it
was a gamble, with the odds against comfort.

Meanwhile, between medieval England and the changing
economic outlook of Ogilby's survey, a different road system had come into being, which clearly coincided with the
growing recognition of London as the unchallenged metropolis of all England. To Ogilby, at any rate, the comparative
novelty of this fact is disclosed by the almost aggresive
attitude he takes to proclaim it. This in turn had coincided with the decline in importance of both Winchester and
Southampton – the wool trade, the Italian merchantmen,
the import of French wines that had made the southern port
of such significance, all had vanished by Ogilby's time. He
in fact caught the two cities at about the lowest ebb of
their distinguished history, broken by the plague and unaware that in bidding farewell to the Pilgrim Fathers they
had sponsored a greater act of history than anything they
had performed hitherto.

To motoring eyes, which see the London-Southampton
road as a choice between the trunk route by Staines and
Basingstoke and the lesser one by Guildford and Farnham,
the Ogilby road seems a curious thing, swinging from one
to the other. Nevertheless it was destined to remain the

premier coach road until horse transport was lost to the railways.

It had deserted the original Saxon route via Guildford to Farnham, but still ran through Farnham, which it reached by Staines and Bagshot. This seems reasonable. London's interests southward from at any rate Tudor times would not have been towards Guildford and Portsmouth, but towards the west, Devon and Somerset. There was only one metropolitan bridge over the Thames, well downstream, while the old Roman road to Staines had probably never gone out of use. By concentrating its efforts on this partly Roman hardway, London was encouraging the fullest use of an exit that led to the south-western ports from Bristol all the way round to Falmouth and Southampton. Since Winchester was no longer a paramount transport centre and the construction of a main road from Winchester to Basingstoke was a thing of the future, a shorter Land's End route could be developed via Staines, Basingstoke and Salisbury; while the more easterly ports like Poole and Lymington and Southampton could be included in the scheme by a link between Farnham on the old road and Bagshot on the new.

LONDON TO BAGSHOT

In the 1600s, then, and probably for a century or more before that, the main road to Southampton left Cornhill in the City, proceeded along the Strand, 'Hay-Market' and 'Pickadilly', crossed the stream at 'Knight's Bridge', the Counters bridge of brick near the present Earls Court road, the wood bridge at Hammersmith, two unspecified and one stone bridge at Brentford, Baber bridge beyond Hounslow (with the sword mills on one side and the powder mills on the other), a wooden bridge at Bedfont, a ford, and finally the wooden bridges at Staines over the Thames.

This list of all those watery hazards, which must still exist underground, typifies vividly the sort of conditions our predecessors took as normal. No wonder that those

who repaired bridges in monastic days were granted spiri-
tual benefits. The road so far, as detailed by Ogilby, was
part of the Land's End route which in his time was reckoned
by the Post Office as one of their six principal roads of England, 'affording in general a very good road as any in the
kingdom, and as good entertainment'. At Staines (with
'several good inns as the George, Lyon etc') the road crossed
the Thames 'over a wooden bridge which is maintained
by a certain toll on wagons, cattle etc that pass over it, and
barges etc that pass under it'. Wooden bridges were common on the Thames because their shape was suited to the
great volume of barge traffic.

After leaving the medieval causeway and the shelter of
Egham, the road climbed up to the open heath, mile after
miserable mile of it. It was one of the most detested regions
in England – Defoe, Fiennes, on to Jane Austen and Cobbett, they all saw it as the abomination of desolation. But
to understand the communications picture till the Railway
Age, it is important to sense how this vast tract covered
the fringes of Berkshire, Hampshire and Surrey, which have
become sought-after townships such as Wokingham, Fleet,
Windlesham and Hindhead. There was no alternative, and
a way had to be found that missed the bogs, was not too
hilly and remained dry in most weathers, despite the sand-
storms.

Ogilby showed an empty void between Egham and Bagshot, except for the New England Inn at what is now Virginia Water, on the other side of the road to the modern
Wheatsheaf. Bagshot, or just beyond, was the parting of
the ways as it still is, the major Land's End road continuing
its doleful path to Basingstoke, the minor Southampton
road its sorry course to Farnham.

As to its other qualities, a famous contemporary of Ogilby stands witness. In 1685 John Evelyn the diarist used it
to wait on James II at Winchester, in the company of his
good friend Pepys. (Alas, Pepys' failing eyesight had already brought his own diary to its close.) From London
they 'tooke coach and six horses, late after dinner, yet got

to Bagshot that night', with time for Evelyn to pay a social
visit in the park while supper was being prepared. 'The next
morning setting out early, we Ariv'd soon enough at Winchester.'

BAGSHOT TO FARNHAM

The Bagshot–Farnham stretch, which is substantially the
A325 that is followed today, has long been a subject of
speculation. Tradition has given it a Roman origin, and
there are signs of pre-Roman occupation. Even before the
military incursions 100 years ago, the whole of the vast heath
was a jumble of tracks. It could well have become a recognized route in medieval times for kings and prelates, when
there was so much contact with places such as Winchester
and Windsor which must have lain through such townships
as Bagshot and Farnham.

Here again the Gough map of 1360 provided corrobora-
tive support. It is accepted that places shown on it which
were not on one of its marked roads would normally be on
important but unmarked roads. Thus it showed Bagshot
linking Windsor Castle and Farnham, but did not suggest
that Bagshot was linked with London, as it omitted Staines.

The road deliberately avoided the Saxon villages of Cove,
Farnborough and Aldershot, which rather confirms the
opinion that its final course came quite late, following a
trend often found with medieval roads (possibly to preserve
the village street), that unless there are definite posting facilities the main highway is taken away from the village. Here
is Defoe (early 1700s) on this exact stretch of Bagshot
Heath: '... horrid and frightful to look on ... I was so far
in danger of smothering with the clouds of sand that I could
neither keep it out of my mouth, nose or eyes ...'

Since it is a common error to believe that the Aldershot
area was unheard of till it became an Army training
ground, it seems right to emphasize that it was in fact well
known through many an earlier century to countless travellers on the main Southampton road. The Army in fact

had its Major-General Grant living in Farnborough way back in the 1790s. It was certainly popular with highwaymen, and two of its inns have been linked romantically with Dick Turpin, though in fact he was a low form of petty thief who was probably never in Hampshire at all.

It has been suggested that the Tumbledown Dick at Farnborough was renamed in his memory, though a more likely tale associates it with Cromwell's son Richard who resigned the Protectorship to become the affable squire of Hursley near Winchester. The latter tradition warrants repetition because it endorses the forgotten fact of the antiquity of the route; whatever its name, an inn at this spot would have been used to serving the best known in the land, and Dick Cromwell with his constant visits to Hampshire could have been a regular customer. The other inn wrongly associated with Turpin, though it was certainly renamed after a local highwayman, is the one that has been rebuilt at the new roundabout where the A325 leaves the Bagshot–Camberley A30. Nowadays it is called the Jolly Farmer, but on the old maps and coaching guides it is always the Golden Farmer, and it seems a great pity that it does not revert to its earlier name. For the golden farmer really was a local farmer who became noted for his generosity in the local inn; inevitably there were curious-minded people who queried the source of his wealth, and in due course he had to swing for it. A similar tale was known in Wiltshire.

It is odd that no less than three misnamings must be recorded at this one place, the junction of the Land's End and Southampton roads. Apart from the Jolly Farmer, there is the apparent misuse of the road-name Maulthway on Chobham Ridges which should more properly be applied to a point about a mile away (see preceding chapter); while finally it is to be noticed that the old Southampton road, where it leaves the Jolly Farmer roundabout and becomes the A325, is called the Portsmouth road. The reason for this change of terminus is discussed in Chapter 9, section 'The New Portsmouth road through Farnham', but it was a very mushroom reason of the 1800s that had no permanence and would barely be recognized today.

After the heath and its sandy hazards, the traveller would have been grateful enough to reach the lush comforts of Farnham (Illus. 8). Even now, when the onetime importance of the Farnborough–Bagshot route has long passed from memory, a glance at the northern end of the town's exits will show how the main fork to the right for the Hog's Back still looks far less important than the minor Farnborough fork to the left, which was the old main road. To complete the picture, it should really go back to that earlier medieval age when the main fork once again turned right for Guildford, though people would not have troubled to make the steep and chilly climb to the Hog's Back unless conditions insisted. They would more likely have kept to the lower southern road through Puttenham which was ancient even when the Saxons found it, the North Downs route that is known in Hampshire as the Harroway. In Surrey and Kent it has been given the misleading name of Pilgrims Way, which ignores its pre-historic origin.

The Hog's Back is so well known to motorists that it deserves a further mention when at this moment it is being given fresh shape with dual carriageways. Among the millions who have traversed it or picnicked on the great stretch of grass verge that runs on each side of the steep ridge on which it stands, how many have remarked on the hedge which, so to speak, prevents the wanderer from falling over the edge of the cliff? It is remarkable to find that these hedge boundaries go back at any rate to the 1600s, when the whole of the area between was recognized as the road.

FARNHAM TO ALTON

This endeavour to retrace the old Southampton road must so far have appeared confusing enough; it has been a matter of re-opening long lost paths and clearing the ground as it is reached. It is a relief to face the next short stretch between Farnham and Alton, for here is something which has been in use as a main road from earliest times. And there are not so many stretches for which that claim can be made. During the whole of that period, certainly for the past 1,000 years, it could have justified another claim that has been made for it, that it was the loveliest ten miles in England; while of that same ten miles A. Young, the agriculturist, was writing in 1767, 'I will beg you will take notice of the fences on each side of the road: I never beheld anything equal to them'. Whether such claims would be upheld today is a matter of doubt, for the 1963 dual carriageway distorted the balance and the perspective which man and nature had evolved over centuries.

The very first line of the road, up to Roman times, would have taken it along the ridge top parallel to the River Wey, an extension of the Harroway. From Saxon times the course of the road, as Ogilby shows, took it rather higher up the slope of the valley than now, through the villages instead of below them. The present line seems to have come about in the early 1700s, probably in advance of the final turnpike road. The Ogilby 1675 road evidently followed the medieval way, for some 200 years before him, in 1467, there is a record of a bequest of ten pounds 'for the reparation of the bad and imperfect road, commencing from the hill on this side of the cross called Froyle Cross to the end of the town of Farnham'.

But while the historic Southampton road journeyed between Farnham and Alton along the north bank of the River Wey, it is important to take note of the forgotten south-bank route which must be just as old, possibly older. This runs from Binsted, the one-time 'capital' of the great hunting forests of Alice Holt and Wolmer, through the Worldham hamlets and so to Alton or Selborne. It was an area that was well exploited in Roman-British days for pottery-making and continued as a royal hunting centre almost to modern times. The way westward from West Worldham, by Farringdon and Ropley to Bishops Sutton and Winchester, must have been in steady use by our earlier monarchs and their attendants.

ALTON TO ALRESFORD

As has been seen, the London–Southampton road was a hotch-potch, a joining up of odd stretches which originally had nothing to do with linking the two termini. Already the way has met three such stretches, from London to Bagshot, thence to Farnham, and again to Alton. There are more to come.

Today's main A31 road from Alton to New Alresford, by Chawton, Four Marks Hill, Ropley Dean and Bishops Sutton, is a turnpike creation of no significance, a juvenile barely 200 years of age. The one it replaced, as the locals complained at the time, was shorter and pleasanter, described later by Cobbett as 'this lofty land which is, perhaps, the finest beechwood in all England'. Parts of it are still in use as minor ways, though the making of the Alton–Alresford–Winchester railway in 1865 would have had a destructive effect on its course through Chawton Park Wood.

The memory of the old road still lingers on, if in distorted fashion. Its most likely origin can be found some 1,500 years ago, when the invading Saxons had made their little river settlements up to the head of the Wey at Alton and the head of the Alre at Bighton. The time had come when one side or both, in amity or enmity, must push its scouts over the hill between to find what lay on the other slope.

The modern A31 through Alton comes to the Butts, which it keeps on its right as it makes a sharp left turn to Chawton village. The more direct old road went straight on with the Butts on its left, along the lane by what is now the Treloar Hospital to a point where it is joined by another lane from the left. Here it forked to the left of the two modern cottages, along what is now an overgrown footpath. After a few yards the footpath opens out in unforgettable manner. Not so long ago it was downland, but the grass, the thyme and the harebells are being rapidly scrubbed out; now it is a jungle of wild life, including adders. But here is the course of the old road, turfed and parallel to the railway, very wide in true medieval fashion. On the left or southern side it is still level enough to have taken wheeled traffic. In places there are at least eight parallel trackways, perhaps a unique survival. It is fitting that they should remain at this place, at the foot of the Pass of Alton in Chawton Park Wood, of which a declaration was made in 1262 :

Further the bishops and other magnates agreed that if the king were pleased to make a clearance of his wood they also would do the same and bring into cultivation all their woods upon the passus making a broad and good highway from Aulton to Alresford.

On its right the old highway becomes two deep and wide sunken ditches with a broad ridge between, almost like the tracks of some gigantic tractor. Though each of these ditches might have constituted a roadway, no normal team of horses could have maintained progress along it, and the suggestion was once made that the ruts might have been made in hauling logs, perhaps on sledges. There is tradition to support such a view. Chawton Park Wood was a great supplier of timber for the Navy; many of the seventeenth- or eighteenth-century houses in the village are said to be framed with old ships' timbers brought back in exchange. The haulage of timber for the shipyards was then the biggest transport problem of its day, with teams of twenty oxen taking a year or more to reach their destination. Whatever the cause, the whole appearance of the old highway is a remarkable witness to past travel which deserves preservation.

Stukeley's reference to traces of a Roman road between Farnham and Winchester is well known. He was probably mistaken, but not in the manner suggested by his detractors, who so often assumed that the road he was following was the modern one. Stukeley, at any rate between Alton and Alresford, would have been riding, in 1723, the pre-turnpike way now being described, and his remarks exactly accord with the evidence which has just been given. The road, he wrote, was

... horribly out of repair, and even in the midst of summer very bad, notwithstanding such plenty of materials everywhere to mend it: this has obliged coaches and horsemen frequently to make excursions for their ease and safety.

What is so remarkable is the continuity of this 'Roman' tradition. A few years after Stukeley and others were noting it, the road was neglected when the new turnpike was built. Today, 200 years later, the existence of the road is all but forgotten and the land here, known to and used by pre-motoring generations as Chawton Common, seems to have passed into private hands. Yet this particular short stretch has been recorded to the author within the past year by two witnesses; a former Sister at the Treloar Hospital and a landowner whose family till lately was long established around Alton. In both cases the tradition was the same; it was 'the old Roman road'. But let it be remembered that 'Roman', which archaeology has made such a closely-defined word, had previously a much wider significance.

Fairness demands one further quotation which suggests a different state of affairs, but no doubt in this case there was a local bias. At any rate a resident (late 1700s) of Old Alresford, Sir George Rodney, recorded some memories of this same road which,

since the turnpike road through Bishops Sutton took place, about the year 1753, has been disused as the London road. The Bishop's copyhold tenants of Old Alresford and Medstead are obliged by their tenures to keep it in repair in district lots, and the several allotments are so particularly described in the Court Rolls of the Manor as to ascertain and distinguish the identical spot (and the exact measure thereof) which every particular estate is to maintain.

It is not impossible that the stretches of repaired road were those mistaken by Stukeley and other contemporary travellers as Roman (subsequently thrown on the parish and repaired 'in the same manner as their other public roads').

A further glimpse of Wessex – or English – history can be found by a return to the main A31 road, where about halfway up the long Four Marks Hill a small lane on the right leads under the railway bridge. The track to be seen just beyond is probably on the line of the old road, and lies in the infamous Pass of Alton which 700 years ago was of such ill-repute for its robbers and footpads that, following the declaration of 1262, a Royal Commission was set up to inquire into it. This led to the renowned Statute of Winchester in 1285 which ordained that the land on either side of the highway must be kept clear to a depth of 200 ft. Up the hill stands another forgotten reminder in Gibbet Copse.

The old road can be met again from the turning off the A31 at the top of Four Marks Hill by the Windmill Inn (in the 1750s it was the 'old windmill stone'), which crosses the railway bridge and shortly after turns sharp left. This left-hand stretch is a made-up section of the old road, and its track through the wood down towards Alton can be seen to the right. The road proceeded, south of Medstead, very much as it does today, by Five Ash Pond towards Bighton, the chief route running south of Goatacre with an alternative through Soldridge. Most of the old ways are no longer made up, but they are easy to trace with their links from one track to the other, even yet with a fantastic width from hedgerow to hedgerow; the whole area a living memorial to the urgent importance of the road when men tramped it en route to Crécy and Agincourt.

At Bighton the original Saxon way swings off beyond the church to Old Alresford, Abbotstone and Winchester. The Southampton route clearly coincides here with the making of the Norman pond, about 1200. The modern lane from Bighton takes a rather higher line than the one adjoining the Alre stream shown by Ogilby. The course of his route can still be followed, past some Tudor cottages on the outskirts of Bighton, and then so close to the water that at one point it actually 'goes through it' as he described. The road continues alongside the pond, over the famous Norman causeways and so to New Alresford by Broad Street.

There is a tradition here of a George Inn that was rebuilt in 1418 to replace an earlier hostelry named the Angel or more popularly the Broadgate. A George Inn certainly stood within the memory of some now living, where the Westminster Bank is located. It might well have been the inn where Leland, about 1540, gathered some typically vague information. But he did have this charming passage:

> Alresford river beginnith of a great numbre of fair sylver springes a good mile above Alresford: and these resorting to a botom make a great brode lak, communely caullid Alsford Pond. Then it cummith into a narow botom and rennith through a stone bridge at the ende of Alresford toun.

NEW ALRESFORD TO TWYFORD

Among the major economic enterprises undertaken by the Norman bishops of Winchester was the development of several new towns as centres for the wool industry. One of them, in the early 1200s, was New Alresford, which paid off well, and, with Winchester and Southampton, waxed fatter and fatter. More and more vessels came to Southampton; there were the French prelates supervising their acquired English properties; the growing Continental trade, as far as Venice; the swelling ranks of pilgrims; finally the great armies that were sent abroad to justify the kingship of England and France.

The inland traffic northwards through New Alresford became too big to be filtered along the Itchen to Winchester, and the capital city had to be bypassed; the advantage of this first bypass being that it provided a much shorter cut, not a longer one as is the current manner. The direct way from Southampton to New Alresford ran via Twyford to

Morestead and over Fawley Down, and, from the barrows and other evidence that bestride its passage, tracks from the Itchen crossing at Twyford may have led in pre-Roman times to other crossings at Itchen Stoke and Tichborne. But now it must be attracted to New Alresford, and no doubt the townsfolk there would have been eager to help create the crossing that is known today as Sewards Bridge, the one-time ford at Sewers Water.

When did this happen? It would be useful to know, because it is this stretch that really dates the London–Southampton road, which up to now has been using the earlier Winchester road. It is shown in route books of the 1500s, though not on the Gough map of the 1300s The latter is not conclusive, and it could well be that troop movements alone would have forced its recognition by then. But it would not be earlier than the arrival of New Alresford, and that suggests a date, say, in the mid-1200s, perhaps with a king like Henry III who was at least roadminded, as is evidenced by his Royal Commission on the Pass of Alton. Even so, until the roles were reversed a century or two later, the route would have originally been known as a branch off the Winchester road.

The road left New Alresford on what is now the dual-carriage A31 to Winchester and crossed the Itchen at Sewards Bridge. The crossing was a ford till the bridge was built in the late 1600s. In a matter of some two miles the venerable Matterly Farm, near which they once put the turnpike tollgate to discourage people from using the Twyford road, stands on the left. It makes a startling comparison to see the old narrow road by the farm against the great dual carriageway, but it must not be ignored. When after another mile or so the A31 turns right, the little road carries on, unsignposted but made up. That is the original Southampton route. Much of the way between this point and the modern A272 Winchester–Petersfield road, which bisects it at right angles, has recently been closed. The author, with no foreknowledge of what was about to take place, made the journey by car on a wettish winter's day in November 1963 and wrote his notes immediately afterwards. They are reproduced in this personal form as a record of probably the last passage that was made of this old historic thoroughfare:

When I made the trip I was unprepared in the sense that I had no modern Ordnance map with me [where the road is still clearly shown]; only the memory of an 18th-century map. But though the made-up section soon faded out, the way was perfectly straightforward, if somewhat damp.

I reached the high ridge of the downs overlooking Temple Valley, thinking of all the characters up to 200 years ago who had stopped here for a look and a breather. There were a couple of gates which respected the Queen's highway and opened to my touch, but beyond the second gate my car took exception to a bad patch of mud. It was anybody's guess whether I should return the way I had come (if I could) when suddenly the tyres gripped again. I found I was on a slight slope and the only way I could maintain the grip was on the downland parallel to and slightly below the banked-up level of the road.

I went ahead for some hundreds of yards, concentrating as one does on the ground immediately in front of me. Suddenly things happened. Something made me look up, and I found that not far in front of me a procession of cars was sailing by. I was annoyed, because there was no road in such a place on my map. Then I realised that my mental map was 200 years old, and the A272 to Petersfield had been built since then.

It was quite a shock, but nothing to the shock that came almost simultaneously. The car decided that it could go neither forward nor backward, and for the first time I had a real look round. I found the old embanked road on my left was way up above the roof: I found the car was heeling over at a most peculiar angle: I found I could gaze downwards to my right, almost to a sheer drop of some hundreds of feet. Then I knew where I was. The cars in front were enjoying the famous view from Cheesefoot Head. Inadvertently I had become part of the entertainment. I was suspended over the Devil's Punchbowl.

Eventually, thanks to the discovery of an outstanding sportsman with a land-rover, I was not only able to have my car hauled out but to cover the remaining unmade-up section to Morestead as well. From Morestead to Twyford it is a built-up road again.

Now for the sequel. The strongly embanked roadway near which I had come to a full stop seemed worthy of recording – it is unusual for a medieval road to show such signs of deliberate making-up 'miles from anywhere'. In the year after my trip, therefore, a photographer and I went to Cheesefoot Head with the intention of walking along the old road for a close-up shot. I found that the gate entrance from the A272 to this 700-year-old highway had been fenced in, and an alternative new bridle path opened up in a different direction. In 2100 a later Stukeley may find the embankment and decide it is Roman. Perhaps it is!

TWYFORD TO SOUTHAMPTON

The old road continued more or less along the present A335, with alternative bridges at Highbridge (Allbrook) and Bishopstoke. At Allbrook it was joined by the Saxon main road from Winchester to Southampton, which in typical fashion had kept to the Roman hardway while it was close to the river, and had then broken away at Otterbourne. References to its upkeep can be traced as far back as the 1300s. The crossing at Mansbridge is mentioned over 1,000 years ago. In 1403 people were offered forty days' indulgence to repair the highway there. The present main road through Chandlers Ford was a minor erratic affair till it was straightened out in Georgian times; the Chandlers Ford bypass was opened in December 1967.

At Eastleigh the road was rather pushed on one side to make room for the railway and its nineteenth-century workshops. The name is often thought to be coincident with the railway town; in fact East Ley Farm, which was standing until a few years ago and may have been built on the foundations of the Roman road, appears on all the old maps long before George Stephenson was born. Its grounds can be seen from the town hall. Originally the railway station was called Bishopstoke, after the local village, and the name was only changed because of confusion with the other Hampshire railway junction at Basingstoke.

The road finished its journey by Swaythling, South Stoneham and Portswood, having by Ogilby's 1675 reckoning covered seventy-eight miles from Cornhill in the City of London. Miss Fiennes was there soon after, noting the depressed state of the town though it was still very clean, 'kept so by their carrying all their carriages on sleds and permit no carts'. At the same time Mr Pepys was finding a similar practice in Bristol, where only dog-carts were allowed, but he gave a more practical reason. The vaults beneath the roadways would have collapsed under heavy traffic.

Pepys did go to Southampton (Illus. 19), riding over from Gosport, and had a royal welcome. 'We went to the Mayor's, and there dined, and had sturgeon of their own catching the last week, which do not happen in twenty years, and it was well ordered.'

CHAPTER FIVE

Berkshire and the Thames

SILCHESTER

BERKSHIRE, with the Thames at Old Windsor, Reading, Wallingford and Dorchester, should be an enthralling hunting-ground for early road systems. In fact it is disappointingly devoid of their traces. Mostly the reason must lie in the Thames itself, which till last century was as important a traffic route as any in the country. A further reason is perhaps to be found in the very earliness of the connexion of Berkshire with Wessex, which was at its peak in the times of the Saxon incursions and since then has tended to fade away. The royal prerogative of Windsor Park would also have led to a disappearnce of earlier routes linking with Winchester, in effect from the line of the Thames by Windsor across to Virginia Water on the Surrey border and along by Bagshot to Sandhurst on the Hampshire border.

The first link that definitely relates Berkshire to the traditional Wessex comes in one of its earliest and most important historical episodes. It concerns the re-establishment of Christianity in England, an event so momentous that the fact is sometimes jeopardized by local myth. The story centres on Dorchester, by the Thames, just south of Oxford. Dorchester was a Roman township on the road from Silchester to the Midlands, though much of its route between these two towns is still lost. It can be traced from Dorchester south through Brightwell to the outskirts of Streatley, where it vanishes till re-emerging just north of Silchester (Illus. 10). The general theory (see, for example, I. D. Margary's *Roman Roads in Britain*) is that it roughly pioneered the path of the present road north to Pangbourne and then followed the river to Streatley.

In this connexion Rocque's big-scale Berkshire map of 1752 is well worth studying. From Dorchester, the course is clear enough in the section south to the edge of Streatley. Then going north from Silchester (which is just inside the Hampshire boundary and is not shown) the line can be picked up almost from the town walls. At any rate it looks like the line, which can also be seen on the early Ordnance Survey drawings of about 1805. But this line on reaching Upton Nivet, where a firm Roman clue has been established, takes a slight inclination to the left, so that instead of aiming for Pangbourne it crosses the Kennet at 'Jack Boot Tile Mill'. This would lead to a crossing of the Pang between Bradfield and Stanford Dingley and so to the old hundred boundary (see Rocque's small-scale index map) which turns north over the hill to link up with the known clues outside Streatley.

But these armchair speculations do not alter the fact that this Roman road led from Dorchester to Silchester and on to Winchester and Southampton. It explains very simply how it was that the first Bishop of Wessex had his see at Dorchester. In 634, says the Anglo-Saxon Chronicle, 'Bishop Birinus preached Christianity to the West Saxons under King Cynegils' and the following year Cynegils was baptized by Birinus, Bishop of Dorchester, and Oswald, King of Northumbria, stood sponsor for him. Now let the Venerable Bede fill in some detail. Birinus, encouraged by Pope Honorius, set out to preach the faith in those parts of Britain which had not yet been converted by the earlier efforts of Augustine. Birinus, with considerable pluck, 'first entered the nation of the West Saxons, and finding all there most confirmed pagans' decided to start his mission there and then.

Birinus, it would seem, had disembarked at the port of the West Saxons. the future Southampton. Naturally he would have inquired for the king. But the king, as Birinus pursued his long and hazardous path along the old Roman road northwards, was not at his Winchester palace. The king had proceeded to the very boundaries of Wessex, across the Thames, to discuss business with King Oswald of Northumbria, his powerful fellow member of the Heptarchy, who was already a Christian. Thus it was at Dorchester that the bishop eventually found Cynegils who was duly baptized in the presence of Oswald, the latter being so delighted that he adopted Cynegils as his son. Then 'the two kings gave to the bishop the city called Dorchester, there to settle his episcopal see'.

Dorchester was not to enjoy episcopal status for long. It was most badly sited to administer the affairs of Wessex, and it was natural for the work to be transferred to Winchester and Sherborne. But it is a tale which can only be strengthened by being linked with the Southampton–Silchester Roman road, the northern end of which even at that time may have been wearing a bit thin for lack of use.

But was it? Upwards of 500 years later, about 1200, King John was scouring Wessex for fresh hunting-grounds. His detailed itineraries are on record, though they do not disclose that a king's movements would involve similar and frequent movements of his considerable personnel, probably including rough, two-wheel baggage carts. How did he get, from Windsor or London, to his favourite resorts of Marlborough, Freemantle near Basingstoke, Ludgershall near Tidworth, Cranborne south of Sarum, except by the Silchester road and one or other of the western Roman roads from Silchester? It was their presence which so obviously determined the siting of these royal resorts. Another suspected royal hunting-lodge, East Worldham, near Alton in Hampshire, presents the same picture of a Roman approach route from Silchester. The conclusion cannot be resisted that, however the routes may have become twisted and distorted, the existence of Silchester as a road centre was recognized through Norman and Plantagenet times, even if its own services were reducd to a wayside smithy. The locating in very recent years of this last-mentioned route from Silchester via East Worldham to Chichester is a great stimulus to the study of past records in tracing Roman antiques. Stukeley's 1723 plan of Chichester for example, actually shows the road, though he not unreasonably thought it went to Winchester.

ROADS FROM OXFORD

The importance of Dorchester diminished in proportion to the growth of its upstream neighbour Oxford, which was to become a key link with the south-west from the Midlands and North. In the 1300s it ranked among the top ten provincial towns. Was it chance that saw Oxford developing on a site which is almost on a straight line due north of Southampton, Winchester and Newbury, with the country just south-west of Newbury an all but impassable jumble of hills and forest? It is interesting to note the recognition of these Oxford routes that was given by John Ogilby in his reappraisal of the main road system in 1675. From Oxford he showed southern roads to Hungerford-Salisbury–Poole, Newbury–Basingstoke–Chichester, Faringdon–Malmesbury–Bristol.

There is little variance in their more northerly lines. The Salisbury road 'affording no very good road to Hungerford, thence indifferent' proceeded to Abingdon, Drayton and Steventon, but then took the downland way that leads over to Farnborough. From there the route went through Great Shefford to Hungerford, whence the modern A338 does not vary greatly from the old road.

The Basingstoke–Chichester road described as 'in general indifferent good' also left Oxford by Abingdon but branched off between Drayton and Sutton Courtney to Milton; whence an 'extraordinary dirty lane' led to Harwell and Chilton, where it is unexpected to find a note, long before the tourist habit developed, saying 'a great vale called the Vale of White Horse or Berkshire Vale'; so back to the line of the A34 north of East Ilsley and on to Newbury. It continued to Basingstoke by Knightsbridge over the Enborne, passing Benham Court (as it was) and the church at

'Stottens', which seems to have disappeared. Its route through Kingsclere and so to Basingstoke is substantially the A339 that is followed today.

The next stage, between Basingstoke and Alton, seems always to have been tenuous, and remained in that state till the latter part of the 1700s. To the historian this early route is not without interest, because it brings out how fully the Harroway was employed until quite recently. The first available record of the 1600s followed the A339 from Basingstoke, keeping west of Hackwood, through Winslade and by Herriard church until it reached the end of the park. Here was a crossroads with the old road coming up from Winchester across the Itchen through Wield and on to Odiham. What is so interesting is that Ogilby's survey was fully accurate on the destinations of this north–south course, though he was not far from being lost on the west–east route he was describing.

Just about here (Nash's Green) the route joined the high-level loop of the Harroway. All Ogilby could find to locate his whereabouts was that you passed 'through a scattering village, an indirect way by some dispersed house, to Alton'. What he was actually doing was to travel from Nash's Green across Weston Common to the Golden Pot, and down the old Odiham to Alton road. An unexpected relic of this 'scattering village' can be found in a few Tudor cottages off the main road in what nowadays is called 'Back Lane' leading to Lasham. 'Back Lane' is an apt description in relation to the modern main road, but it might once have been 'Pack Lane', a name met farther west on the Harroway at Kempshott. Ogilby hinted at an alternative route and this seems to have become the recognized way by the mid-1700s. It left Basingstoke, joined the low-level loop of the Harroway north of Hackwood and then branched off through Tunworth, keeping west of Weston Corbett to join the first route near the Golden Pot. The remainder of this route from Alton to Chichester is discussed in Chapter 9, 'To Portsmouth from the Midlands'.

Ogilby included one more Midland route, that coming

down from Chipping Camden in the Cotswolds, through
Burford and Marlborough, to Salisbury: a delightful run,
which his surveyor seemed to linger over. But after Marlborough the joys of the open road took him by a most circuitous route, through Savernake to Burbage, then cutting
across to Everleigh where he noted a 'False Stone' in the
neighbourhood of Oldhat Barrow which, by the mid-1700s
had become 'Ballstone Pond', and by 1800 'Falston Bottom'. The way proceeded by some indefinable route across
the plain that met neither village nor stream until it reached
Old Sarum. It was the 'old Marlborough Way' that branches
north-east near Durnford off the A345 from Salisbury and
runs through Bulford – it became a turnpike.

Seekers of pre-Roman trackways will be interested to
compare this circuitous Ogilby route with the more direct
pre-Roman one, given in Timperley and Brill's *Ancient
Trackways of Wessex*, that travels from Everleigh on the
plain, north of Easton and Ram Alley. The use of this
route as a throughway to the Midlands and North is interesting, especially in view of Ogilby's apparently con-
temptuous ignoring of the main east–west trackways such
as the Ridgeway and the Icknield Way over which these
Berkshire roads have passed. Perhaps his was a time, just
prior to the London cattle-droving period, when the old
ridgeways were comparatively unused.

It is indeed disappointing that in a county like Berkshire,
so intimately associated with the foundations of England –
with Wessex and Wantage, Wallingford and Windsor –
there is so little trace of its more southerly communications
with Winchester. The struggles raged there in the early
Saxon incursions and they continued there when the country was united against the Danes. The simple fact is that
there are so many routes over the downs, of all ages and
compass bearings, that the lines were always open southward from the Thames. It has often been noted that social
inclinations of peoples tend to urge them to the west and,
in the northern hemisphere, to the south. This was as true
when the Continental invaders turned to Cranborne Chase

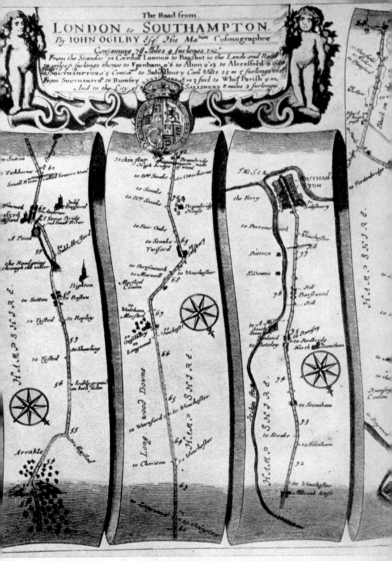

1. Section of scroll map by John Ogilby, 1675, London–Southampton road. Bottom left column shows old route from Alton through Chawton Park Wood; bottom centre the cross road Winchester–Cheriton–Petersfield

2. Horsebridge on the Test. The rejected Andover–Southampton railway was built along the route of the rejected Andover–Southampton canal: the line of the rejected Roman Winchester–Old Sarum road and its crossing of the Test is given by the signals and trees

3. Ringwood, Hampshire, in 1967. The first 200 years of this period brought an extension to the inn; the motoring age brought the 1936 bypass road and bridge. Major road developments took place in 1968 but the inn survives

4. The Harroway in Hampshire near Oakley (Pack Lane), towards Overton

5. The old main London–Southampton Road descending from Fawley Down to Morestead. See Ogilby map (Illus. 1), centre column, near compass bearing

6. Crossroads below the deserted village of Abbotstone

7. The approaches to Charford on the Hampshire Avon where the Saxons recorded a decisive victory in 519, brought out from long range by a telescopic camera

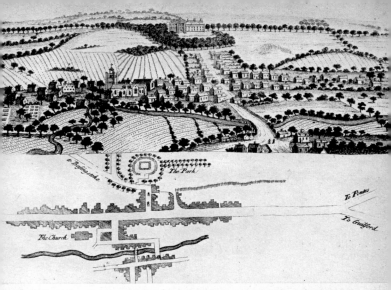

8. Farnham, 1723. Stukeley thought it was the Roman Calleva (Silchester); thus the road through it was held to be the Roman way from Winchester (Venta) to Staines (Pontes) and London

9. Marlborough on the Bath (or Bristol) road, 1723

10. Silchester (its walls pictured in 1722) was badly sited as a Roman road centre and despite heavy state investment was never densely populated

11. The great Norman palace of Clarendon in 1723

12. Seaton, Devonshire, southern terminal of the Fosse, in 1723

Both illustrations show the clifftop routes often favoured by horse-back travellers

13. Lyme Regis, Dorset, 1723, with its famous cobb or pier separated from the shore

14. Bridge Casterton, Dorset, from Hermen Street, 1724

15. Staines and Hythe seen by Wm Stukeley, 1723. The Roman road he described is that from middle left to middle right on the plan

16. The Old Petersfield–Havant–Portsmouth road near Buriton.
Nelson is thought to have used this route on his last English journey
in 1805

17. Approach to Hawkley near Petersfield from the Oxford–Portsmouth road, unaltered since Cobbett vilified it in 1828

18. Approaching Fern Barrow, the old road from the Alum Chine workings at Bournemouth is almost lost to housing development at Coy Pond

19. Southampton in 1723, with apparent raised causeway approach across the Common

20. Winchester in 1723 from St Giles Hill, with east gate and walls standing. Left of west gate (towards top) is the never-completed fabric of Wren's palace for Charles II

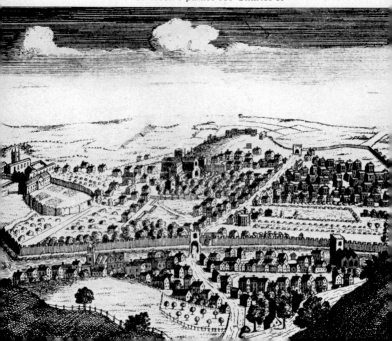

and the New Forest for their relaxation as it is today when people seek Bournemouth and Torquay for their retirement.

Till last century, when the horse ceased to be an essential constituent of social life, old maps and old writings point to the same conclusion: when a man was riding and came to the open downs he just took a point a long way ahead and rode for it. This 'bump of location' is one of the senses that in motoring communities has all but vanished. Pedestrian and horse-riding peoples have it and think nothing of it. Theoretical treatises on how the Romans were able to sight their straight roads ignore the fact that many of them could do the job without any elaborate equipment. In later days, as pocket compasses became available, it was the custom for travellers to take a bearing and ride on it. But in Wessex, with no large rivers to complicate matters, and provided the horseman avoided woodlands, he could not really go far wrong.

Although the routes discussed are mostly those downland passages running southwards from the Thames, by contrast it is useful to read Arthur Young's experiences on the main roads, at a date in the 1760s when the new turnpike system was in its birth pangs. Of the country approaching Oxford on the London–High Wycombe road, he wrote:

From Tetsford [Tetsworth] to Oxford is extremely disagreeable, barren, wild and almost uninhabited. The road called by a vile prostitution of language a turnpike, is all of chalkstone, of which loose ones are everywhere rolling about to lame horses. It is full of holes and the ruts very deep; and withal so narrow that I with great difficulty got my chair out of the way of the Witney wagons and various machines which are perpetually passing. The tolls are very dear ... The road from Witney to North Leach is I think the worst turnpike I ever travelled in. They mend and make with nothing the [local] stone ... which rises in vast flakes, and in pieces as large as one's hand.

The system could easily be improved, noted Young, who found several short stretches of good road, 'done with the same materials, with the only difference of reducing them to very small pieces, not larger than common pebbles, and widening and levelling it'.

What is always surprising is the amount of this travelling that was done at night. Here, for example, 100 years before Young, is Mr Pepys with wife and two friends in a hired carriage. They were travelling from Oxford to Salisbury along one of the routes discussed above, in a period (1668) exactly contemporary with Ogilby's survey. They had spent the night at Abingdon 'where had been a fair custard'. They saw the hospital and

> so to the inn, and paid the reckoning and whatnot, 13s.
> So forth towards Hungerford. Led this way by our land-
> lord ... He gone, we forward; and I vex'd at my people's
> not minding the way. So come to Hungerford

whence, after dinner 'set out with a guide, who saw us to Newmarket-heath, and then left us, 3/6d'. This would probably have been the route noted by Leland in the previous century, through Shalbourne and running down to join the Marlborough Way to Old Sarum. Pepys continued ...

> so all over the plain by the sight of the steeple to Salis-
> bury, by night; but before I came to the town, I saw a
> great fortification ... and find it prodigious, so as to
> fright me to be in it all alone at that time of night, it
> being dark.

This was Old Sarum, as truly described then as though it were today.

It was a day or two later that occurred one of the best-known passages in Pepys on his connubial journeys: 'Up, finding our beds good, but lousy; which made us merry'. The party had left Salisbury about six in the evening, with the usual guide and went over the smooth plain indeed till night; and then by a happy mistake we were carried out of our way to a town where we would lie ... glad of this mistake, because had we gone as we intended, we could not have passed with our coach, and must have lain on the plain all night.

We never learn where it was, only that they arrived next at Norton St Philip.

THE BATH ROAD

Although much of the Bath road is outside the scope of this book, it is perhaps not out of place to have a look at its origin, since in the past 200 or 300 years it has attracted such glamour and panache to its name that it tends to swamp its neighbours. That this is a recent happening can be easily demonstrated. It is the general belief today that the Great West road, the road out of London that was built in the 1920–30s from Chiswick as a bypass of Brentford and Hounslow, is the beginning of the Bath road which proceeds to Slough and Reading. In fact the Great West road historically is the branch that continues to Staines and Basingstoke and Salisbury, as is continually noted in this book. Its alternative name was the Land's End road, just as the Great North road, before the union with Scotland took it over the border, was called Barwick road (a terrible indictment of our modern pronunciation of 'Berrick'). Main roads from London always ended at the water's edge, and it is proper therefore that, as recently as Ogilby's survey of 1675, before Bath had become the extremity of fashion that would shortly follow, the route was not called the Bath road, but the Bristol road. Needless to say, it ignored Bath completely, and took the direct way through Marshfield.

The manner in which a distorted aspect of this original fact has come about can soon be shown. In Ogilby's description of the Land's End road, from London through Staines, he says 'at the end of Hounslow you keep the forward way over Hounslow Heath, omitting the acute way on the right to Colnbrook'. It is the Colnbrook turn that is the start of the Bristol, or Bath, road. Some 225 years later, W. O. Tristram, in his well-known *Coaching Days and Coaching Ways*, 1901, quoted a traveller of 1840 that

> There were eight mails that passed through Hounslow. The Bristol, Bath, Gloucester and Stroud took the right hand road from Hounslow; the Exeter, Yeovil, Poole and Devonport went the straight road towards Staines.

At this very late coaching period the Southampton coach had returned to the original Winchester route through Guildford and Farnham. It is only in the current, motoring, century that the situation has been reversed. Thus C. G. Harper's *Historic and Picturesque Inns of Old England*, 1926, immediately before the Great West road bypass was built:

> The road to Bath and the Exeter road have one common course from Hyde Park Corner until Hounslow is reached. At the end of that town you bear left for Staines and Exeter, or keep straight on for Bath.

It was a long time, after the Saxons had settled themselves in England, before there was likely to have been an important route between London and Bristol. For one thing, the tendency would have been for the pull to have been exercised towards Winchester or Southampton, and in fact the communications between Bristol and the South Coast ports have always received emphasis in old records. Now it has already been seen that till well into medieval times the Great West road was routed to London via Winchester, Farnham and Guildford; the old Roman way via Silchester and Staines being at that stage of lesser importance. What was of supreme importance to the Saxons was the River Thames, which was probably their main method of communication with the Midlands. It was natural therefore for the Roman way from London to Silchester to remain in popular use as far as Staines, and natural for land ways to grow up where they provided serviceable short cuts to the river route. One such land way between Staines and the important Saxon township of Reading, cutting out the long river bend by Maidenhead, can be noted running by Winkfield and Binfield. Another such way came at the convenient crossroads at Hounslow, which provided a land way to the key points at Chertsey and Kingston downstream, and Old Windsor upstream, via Colnbrook. The Ostrich Inn at Colnbrook claimed not only that it was descended from a monastic guest house of 1106, but that its very name could be traced from the original Latin *hospitium*.

The next main upstream crossing of the Thames would have been at Windsor, to reach Reading via Waltham St Lawrence. Stukeley (1723) noted 'Laurence-Waltham, which has been Roman: there is a field called Castlefield, and vast numbers of coins found'. Rocque's *Berkshire Gazetteer* of the mid-1750s agreed.

Wartham Lawrence appears by the several Roman coins that have been dug up here, especially of the latter emperors, and by the ruin of bricks etc to have had once a considerable Roman fort; it stood in a field, now called Weycock, i.e. the high-road, for such were all the Roman ways leading from one fort or garrison to another.

It is interesting that a road between the Roman stations at St Albans and Silchester has long been suspected and a tentative line at St Albans is shown in the Ordnance Survey map of Roman Britain. Such a line, continued to Silchester, would pass close to Waltham St Lawrence. At Silchester Stukeley was told that a stretch of Roman road, not now visible, went to Burghfield and Reading. This would be a reasonable mistake, and it can easily be checked that a very slight variation would take it to Waltham St Lawrence and St Albans, whereas had it been the Dorchester road the variation would seem too great.

At Reading there would be another natural parting of the Saxon ways, the north-westerly one following the Thames, the south-westerly the Kennet, along by Theale, Aldermaston, Newbury, Hungerford and Marlborough (Illus. 9), just south of the old Roman Bath road. These latter towns were of chief importance for their north–south connexions, but thanks to the Kennet the road was able to provide, for some seventeen miles, a straight route with three useful stopping-places. It continued westwards along the old Roman road to Bath, until the river turned north near Avebury. Stukeley (1723) had a most interesting comment about the route west of Marlborough where the Roman road

> meets again the common road near the White-hart ale-house; and so they go together above West Kennet to Silbury Hill: this was the post and coach road to Bath, till, for want of reparation, they were forced to find a new one, more northward upon the downs, and farther about, through the town of Abury: when on the south side of Silbury hill, it goes very strait and full west through the cornfields on the south of Bekhamton, where it is sufficiently known by the name of the French way: for what reason I cannot imagine. They have of late endeavoured to exclude travellers going upon it, by inclosing it at both ends with ditches; but the badness of the lower road has defeated their purpose, and made people still assert the public right.

Here also the paths of the Roman road to Bath and the medieval road to Bristol separated. In 1360 the Gough map showed the Bristol road as one of the only main three roads in the south of England, with no mention of Bath. Even in those remote days Bristol was the most important city, outside London, in southern England, vying with York in the north.

The road ran to Chippenham, going north of Calne, through Marlborough, Hungerford, Newbury, Reading,

Maidenhead, Colnbrook and Brentford. As for the glamorous Bath road, it emerges from this review as a fortuitous thing, arising from the bends of the Thames and the straightness of the Kennet.

CHAPTER SIX

Routes to Somerset

ANDOVER TO ALFRED'S TOWER

OF the major east–west roads that penetrated Wessex, those that demand examination are the most southerly, through Dorchester and Bridport; the most important, through Salisbury and Shaftesbury; and the most northerly, through Reading and Marlborough. To complete the review there should be a road through Andover towards Taunton and Bridgwater in Somerset, and this is suggested by Ogilby in his 1675 route from London to Barnstaple. He took it up at Andover, after it had followed the Land's End route through Staines and Basingstoke, and its adventures on the borders of Wiltshire and Somerset are perplexing. From Andover it followed the present byroad near Abbotts Ann through Monxton, Grateley and Cholderton. Close by was the contemporary home of Miss Celia Fiennes at Newton Tony which, she related 'is all on the downs a fine champion (open) country pleasant for all sports – riding, hunting, coursing, setting and shooting'. Through Amesbury with its bridges, one stone and one wood, the road came to Stonehenge, where it took the right fork.

This is a major variation, for today the road to Taunton, the A303, takes the left fork at Stonehenge and so to Mere and Wincanton. But till the latter part of the 1700s, in Ogilby's time 100 years away, this was wild country, and the traveller, for example, from Salisbury to Taunton would journey up the Wylye valley from Wilton through Hindon, and then ride north of the A303 to that great pre-Roman road, known in Hampshire as the Harroway, which runs along the top of the ridge above Stourhead, past the ruined

Alfred's Tower, and so by Redlynch towards Castle Cary.

The Ogilby route, then, forked right at Stonehenge and made its way to Shrewton, Orcheston St George and Warminster. It took what must have been a magnificent downland route running by Bowls Barrow, south-west of Imber, and came down to Warminster by Boreham. This was one of these great downs roads – in this case from Amesbury to Westbury – that have a record of probably thousands of years of useful work, up to the present century. Unhappily the writer has never been able to visit it, though it may be of some small interest to recall that, some years ago, having seen this route, and the one through Imber, shown as open ways on the then current Ordnance map, he set out to travel that way to London, making the necessary detour to Warminster in order to do so. Following the map he started up Sack Hill, only to be turned back by the military. Shortly afterwards the storm broke about the closing of Imber Down by the then War Office without any apparent authority.

Having reached Warminster, the Ogilby road turned south again, through the suburb of Sambourne to the county boundaries of Somerset and Wiltshire at Maiden Bradley. With thoughts of the stately homes and beauty spots of the 1960s, it is fitting to record that 300 years ago Mr Ogilby noted 'Shearwater Head, a very large spring' and gave a direction to Longleat. Close at hand the other trunk route just mentioned, that through Hindon to cross the present A303 west of Mere at Willoughby Hedge, has joined the prehistoric Harroway by Whitesheet Hill, running along Long Lane south of Kilmington to the top of the ridge at Alfred's Tower. The Ogilby road, most carefully detailed, even to listing Yarnfield and Grange Farm which appear on today's maps, went through the village of Kilmington, across the common, and joined its fellow road at the top of the hill. It is, in fact, by no means a bad spot for rumination, for here, once again, there emerges a medieval road system that far precedes the turnpike period.

At one time the powerful bishops of Winchester owned, amongst other properties outside their see, the towns of Downton and Hindon in Wiltshire and Taunton in Somerset (perhaps whilst Somerton was still the county town). It is always of value, when pursuing the course of these early roads, to check on the outlying properties of monastic establishments, for they can be expected to suggest, or confirm, the line of a route in general use between the two places. This long-distance trek between Winchester and Taunton is as good an illustration as can be found of our national road development. It can be seen how it shows no interest in Roman hard roads, but confines itself to pre-Roman high ground and Saxon valley routes. From Winchester to the first point of Downton, the road started along the old ridgeway, dropped down to the valley of Lockerley, rose along the heights to Redlynch and so to the river at Downton. From there it crossed to Wilton and along the River Nadder to its next point at Hindon where it rose again to the high ground and the old ridgeway on Whitesheet Down through Kilmington Street, to the subsequent site of Alfred's Tower.

Alfred's Tower seems to be missed by the thousands who visit the National Trust show gardens at Stourhead of which it is part. It was erected in the late 1700s, to the constant delight of Parson Woodforde's eyes near Castle Cary, as a memorial to Alfred's defeat of the Danes in 878, on the verge of the famous Penselwood or Selwood Forest. The modern conception of Wessex, thanks to Thomas Hardy, is rather more southerly than this upland that looks towards the Mendips and the Bristol Channel. Yet there is nowhere closer to the heart of the concept of this undefined territory than Selwood. Here are the references to the places in the Anglo-Saxon Chronicle alone. In 645 Cenwalh, King of Wessex, who founded Winchester Cathedral, continued the western advance and at Penselwood drove the British to flight as far as the River Parrett ... In 709 the great Bishop Aldhelm died; his diocese of Sherborne extended 'to the west of the wood', ie, Selwood ... In 878 was that great victory of Alfred's, when he gathered the men of Somerset and Wiltshire and 'that part of Hampshire which was on this side of the sea' (presumably west of Southampton Water or the Isle of Wight); he marched them eastwards and broke up the Danes who gave him hostages and solemn oaths that they would leave the kingdom and promised that their king would receive baptism ... But they came back and in 894 they had reached the Severn, and once again the king's men were assembled from every fortress east of the Parrett, both east and west of Selwood, and in due course starved out and defeated and Danes who were reduced to eating their horses ... Up till 1016 the battles were continued, with King Edmund fighting the Danish host in that long series of engagements all over the south of England which led, after his death and burial at Glastonbury, to the choice of Canute as King of England.

There are more threads to be drawn together, for this is a veritable hotch-potch of roadways, and the remarkable thing is that some of them continued in use right into the coaching period of the last century. Indeed, the only part of the Ogilby road of 1675 which has been re-explored, and which does not appear as some form of main road in the guide books of the early 1800s, is the section across Imber Down which the Ministry of Defence has now sealed off. To study the other essential route hereabouts, it is necessary to return to Amesbury, travel westwards once more to Stonehenge, but take the left-hand fork instead of the right as Ogilby's Warminster route recommended. This left fork is the modern trunk A303 through Mere and Wincanton, and it is most noticeable that Ogilby would have nothing to do with it. Usually so profuse with his crossroad directions, at Stonehenge he remained dumb. About a mile from Amesbury, at the top of the hill, he marked on the right '7 barrows or small hills' and showed a left fork to 'Stoke' (Winterbourne Stoke on the A303). There was no suggestion of a through road. In 1719 appeared a later edition of Ogilby by John Senex 'now improved, very much corrected, and made portable'. Senex had indeed produced a completely new set of most beautiful copperplates – and so portable (the great disadvantage with Ogilby's work was its enormous size) that a horseman could easily pocket the whole book of 100 plates. He had also considered Stonehenge afresh, because he added a recommendation that it was 'worthy the curious Traveller's observation'. But he saw no need to recommend the left fork.

What seems to have gone wrong happened just before Mere. The traveller could no doubt get to Wylye quite smoothly and on to Chicklade and the top of the hill that runs down to Mere. This is the spot, marked on the Ordnance map as Willoughby Hedge, where the Salisbury road through Hindon joins in from the south. This road, as has been seen, continued till recently north of the A303 along the old Harroway to Alfred's Tower, and this is precisely what the left fork from Stonehenge had to do as well. Prior to Stonehenge Ogilby showed an 'unsignposted' left turn that might be an acknowledgement of the very ancient Harroway, which started at Dover or thereabouts and came through Hampshire north of the Test to Amesbury, where it led by Stonehenge, forked left, and somewhere about Chicklade became the line followed by the A303.

There were also a couple of Roman roads in this neighbourhood, the most important road from the Mendip lead mines to Old Sarum and the coast, and the road from Poole Harbour to Bath (or the Mendips) which could have crossed it hereabouts. Traces of both are scanty, perhaps because it was not necessary to make them into hard roads throughout their length – the existing Celtic tracks would be sufficient.

A search through south-west England for an area that represented in its communication lines every phase of history might easily be met by the square mile round Alfred's Tower. No wonder that the county boundaries of Dorset, Somerset and Wiltshire should coalesce there; no wonder the Danes appeared there; no wonder that the modern showplaces of Longleat and Stourhead should have been planted there. But the visitors seem well disciplined, and

most of these early ways can be pursued without distur-
bance. A further study of that big Wiltshire map of the
mid-1700s is revealing. At that time the turnpike system
was in the early stages of its progress, and it shows a most
curious thing. The main coach route from London had
come through Amesbury and had taken the left fork (A303)
at Stonehenge. A glance at the modern map will show how
even now the line of the road there is along the right fork,
as Ogilby had it; the left fork was probably an imposition
of this new turnpike. It continued as far as the top of Charnage Hill or Willoughby Hedge, where it was joined by the
Salisbury road through Hindon, with its tollgate. At this
point, ninety-six miles from London, the original London
turnpike road, as has been seen, continued with its milestones around Whitesheet (north of the A303 to Mere) and
on to the county boundary of Alfred's Tower (104 miles).
The part of the road from Willoughby Hedge towards Kilmington is no longer made up, but at any rate till recently
there was still an old milepost or two along there. There
are also one or two most pretty ones still to be seen on the
Longbridge Deverill–Maiden Bradley–Bruton road, with a
small iron plate on the stone which just shows the mileage
to Bruton. Were these the gift of a local philanthropist?

But the map shows something else, the birth of the A303
as a through road. It was a turnpike extension from Willoughby Hedge down the hill to Mere, but it bore the milestone numberings of the Salisbury–Hindon road until it
reached number 22 at Mere. This was the end of the turnpike – there was no reference to it for the next couple of
miles to the county boundary. Indeed, it is clear that the
improvement to alignment that was necessary between
Zeals and Bourton had not then been carried out. And the
small area of Dorset that here takes over the main road was
able to slumber on, content with its Boundary Stone and its
Green Dragon Inn. So at this point, poised on top of the
ridge for their descent into Somerset, there were in the mid-
1700s two lines of road: the earlier Ogilby route to the north,
that has joined with the later turnpike at the Harroway by

Alfred's Tower on the crest of Kingsettle Hill, and the incipient A303 which has succeeded in descending the hill at Charnage Down but is held uncertainly at Mere.

WHITESHEET HILL

Proof of the importance to the traveller of this small area lies in the considerable records that are available; the reason no doubt is to be found in the steep drop from the open plain to the Somerset dales, represented by Whitesheet and Kingsettle hills. The problem had presented itself from prehistoric times, and the modern map brings out clearly how earlier routes took the Harroway from Stonehenge north-west to Kingsettle Hill, while the later turnpike roads aimed more directly to the west through Mere and Wincanton to Sparkford.

In spite of all that is written, or inferred, in modern books about travelling conditions in the past, the truth of the matter seems to be that for the majority of travellers they were adequate. The simple explanation is that the majority of travellers moved on foot or horseback. It was only when wheeled travel became more general that the complaints started, and it was the wheels that caused the trouble. Thus it can reasonably be said that the state of the roads at the end of the 1600s was far worse than it was in the 1400s; but the reason is not entirely that usually given, of the efficient monastic repair system, but simply that more and more wheeled vehicles were appearing to break up the existing, usually natural, surfaces.

Most of the romantic descriptions of old road conditions are those of the later coaching days; the odds against which the drivers battled were chiefly due to the weather, which can be even more dangerous to a motorist than to a coach passenger, or to hazards such as highwaymen, who also are not unknown in the 1900s and again have nothing to do with the poor state of the roads.

As regards pre-turnpike days, the references to bad surfaces are surprisingly few. Pepys and Evelyn in the mid-

1600s travelled by four- or six-horse coach throughout much of southern England, apparently without harm. It is tempting to conclude that they were getting the best of the pre-wheel network before the wheels destroyed it. And this would explain Young's remark in the 1760s that a bad turnpike road he travelled in his light chaise or 'chair' was a much better one before they started to improve it!

A typical surface for a pre-turnpike road would be that described by Young as a byroad. The water must be carried off, he wrote, and the ruts are single deep channels, lying low in the centre and requiring grips (drains) to let the water off; unless the ruts are single and deep, as in cross roads, grips may be cut for ever without effect; for where there is so much thick mud they are eternally filling up again.

Steep hills have always been the worst opponent of wheeled vehicles, a factor that continues into this century. Cobbett, even when riding the Hampshire lanes in the 1820s, was claiming that the declivities were more dangerous than anything he had met in deepest America, and certainly, in the far West Country, conditions were no easier. Wheeled traffic could get about on the main roads, but anyone who got off them was asking for trouble. The difference between main and minor roads, even in the late 1700s, is well brought out in this description by the anonymous author of *A Tour through the South of England* 1791. His party left the Exeter turnpike at Okehampton on Dartmoor, 'a place supported entirely by its high road and a small manufactory of serge' and then headed north to Barnstaple,

> proceeding over one of the worst roads we had yet encountered, in a post chaise, with four horses, whose drivers told us we might think ourselves well off that they condescended to conduct us at all, and were dragged through Hatherleigh and Torrington.

This in summer!

Here is Ogilby's earlier description of a less important

throughway in Somerset: 'It's an indifferent well-frequented Road, yet a great part of it is a bad, deep way'.
And here, just about the same time (1690) is a description
by Miss Fiennes of this exact Wiltshire/Somerset border.

> From Stonehenge I went to Mere, where is a vast high
> hill called the Castle of Mere, it's now all grass over and
> so steep up that the ascent is by footsteps cut in the side
> of the hill ... from thence to Wincanton which is on a
> steep hill and very stony; you go through the town all
> the way down as it were a steep precipice, all rocks;
> thence to Castle Cary ... as we returned from thence
> we came to Bruton a very neat stone built town, from it
> we ascended a very high steep hill all in a narrow lane
> cut out of the rocks, and the way is all like stone steps;
> the sides are rocks on which grow trees thick, their roots
> run amongst the rocks, and in many places fine clear
> springs bubble out, and run a long way out of the rocks,
> it smells just like the sea: we were full on hour passing
> that hill, though with four horse and a chariot, my Sister
> self and maid; thence to Wylye ...

This can only be Kingsettle Hill on the Harroway, up to
the (later) Alfred's Tower. But there was nothing remarkable about that type of road for horses or pedestrians. They
can be found today as relics of medieval pack-routes. Miss
Fiennes was accustomed to travelling on horseback. From
the context it would seem she rode from Stonehenge to
Castle Cary, then stayed with her sister in the neighbourhood, and they came home together by coach.

Her description of Wincanton is also exactly right. It
makes clear with a few vivid words that the bend southwards which leads towards Sparkford on the A303 is a newcomer, a turnpike introduction. The true road through
Wincanton is that which goes to Castle Cary, A371, and it
is not reached by the left turn in the centre of the town, nor
even the road that runs by the church. Miss Fiennes' steep
precipice will be found to the right or north of the church

road, dropping down to the stream and the Castle Cary road. And how doubly welcome it is today, away from the main traffic. But Wincanton, as seems well brought out in Miss Fiennes' narrative, was not in her day a town on the main London road, which bypassed it to the north from King Alfred's Tower. The Wincanton–Castle Cary road met the main road at the present crossroads of the A371 with the A359, before Castle Cary is reached.

Meanwhile, before Wiltshire is finally left behind, it is worth recording that some fifty years after Miss Fiennes had grappled with her coach up Kingsettle Hill, the old Harroway route by the tower was a turnpike thoroughfare which must have been sound enough to transport George III on one of his return trips from Weymouth, since Fanny Burney mentioned that he visited Redlynch at the foot. It was the first of these roads to become the main London coach route and its exact way can be picked up from the coaching guides of the 1800 period. Paterson, in his London to Barnstaple road, took the road left of Stonehenge, by 'Willey' and Chicklade to Willoughby Hedge, to Kilmington and Hardway. At Willoughby Hedge he had a note saying that you could proceed to Mere, but must rejoin the upper road again before Kilmington. The main trunk Exeter road through Wincanton, the A303, was by this time open, and it is odd that the older route to Castle Cary should still be recommended, cutting out Wincanton. At Hardway he had another note saying you could bypass Bruton and proceed through Shepton Montacute, or take the slightly longer road by Bruton.

Even in Ogilby's time it was noticeable that there was nothing isolated about this Alfred's Tower road. Some hundred years later came the first large-scale map of Somerset (1782, by Day and Masters). By then the turnpike system was in full order, but it is fairly simple to follow Ogilby's directions on the new map, though they may be almost meaningless on a current one. Ogilby – his spelling and wording later corrected by Senex – came down Kingshuttle (Kingsettle) Hill to the Bruham (Brewham) brook, which is obviously the crossing where the Bull Inn now stands. The Bull Inn, with its most unusual retention of an outside stairway, must have witnessed much of what is being discussed. This spot is clearly the hamlet of Hardway shown in the 1782 map and indicated in the coaching guides. It would be interesting to know the evidence on which the Ordnance map gives the Hardway name to the whole length of road from there to the Redlynch crossing. Both the old maps indicate a number of cottages here – far more than today – whilst from Hardway a road ran to Lord Fitz-harding's New Park which seems to have embraced the land around the ruined Stavordale Priory.

It was here, said Stukeley, that men digging a hole for a gatepost came on a piece of lead, with a Roman inscription to Antoninus, weighing 50 lb, which subsequently found its way to Longleat. This finding of the lead, presumably dropped in transit from the Mendips to the coast, is yet one more link in a suggestive chain. The lead was lost, it can be assumed, on a regular through road which continued via Old Sarum to the Winchester road. On this road later appeared the Norman Stavordale Priory, it being a Norman custom to use firm Roman roads when siting their buildings. The Priory stood on a thoroughfare which even today is recorded on the Ordnance map as Cockroad, another ancient description applied to Roman hardways. The word Hardway as applied to the neighbouring hamlet might have referred to a north–south route as well as the east–west one with which it is now associated. To this add the fact that traces of the Roman road from Badbury to Bath or the Mendips are lost a few miles away. Did it or a branch perhaps take this lower route towards Bourton from Donhead St Mary? The B3081 road from Shaftesbury must once have led this way.

The Ogilby route turned off towards Bruton soon after Hardway, coming into the town from the east. Such an entrance shows that the main ways of Bruton are not the real Bruton, which lies around the church and the school and the bridges, a most fair specimen of medieval and Georgian

England. Its relative importance in the later Norman era was recognized by its inclusion, by the symbol drawing of a church, on the Gough map of 1360. Ogilby then took the route to Castle Cary or Ansford by the way through Cole that kept north of Honeywick Hill. Later routes travelled through Pitcombe, which is also bypassed today, though it deserves a quick look – the name is frightening but the old road up towards Hadspen is just about motorable, with care. Pitcombe is the exact original of those pen-and-ink or copperplate drawings that illustrated so many books in the later 1800s, with small girls in long voluminous skirts, and a stream and a bridge and a cottage (always with its smoke), and a cart and horse with its attendant with his trousers tied up at the knee. Pitcombe is all of that and more. Across it, suspended high in the heavens, is the most ethereal railway viaduct, the sort of thing that would have been built by a Roman engineer in France or a Brunel in England. It should have been painted by a Turner or a Monet. It is one of the railways (ex-Somerset and Dorset) which is now closed down, that line from Bath to Poole which ranked as one of the most romantic in Britain.

Thus the road met the Wincanton–Castle Cary A371 where it was left at the crossroads with the A359 near Hadspen House. For at last the various routes from Amesbury have come together again. (The pre-Roman Harroway seems to have forked round towards Cadbury Castle, though it must surely have had a link with the Fosse near Ilchester.) Nowadays there is a cut back by the A359 to Sparkford and the A303, but the true route follows on by Castle Cary.

An important point is brought out in Stukeley's meticulous plan of Ilchester, dated 1723. Where the Fosse makes its island crossing of the 'Ivel' river (the island with 'Little St Mary's Chapel'), the map marked a 'pavement across the river' just west of the Fosse. But it gave no suggestion of the future A303 to Sparkford, which might have been the line of the Harroway. This means that the road from Castle Cary or Bruton to Sparkford (A359) can only have

led south to Sherborne or Yeovil. At the exact point where
the A303 now reaches Ilchester (Northover church) Stukeley's only interest was in Mrs Hoddle's greyhound bitch,
'from whose side a skewer of wood seven inches long had
worked its way out from the stomach'.

The happy little town of Castle Cary tends to be bypassed
by modern roads – which is probably why it is happy – but
at one time there must have been some soreness with its
neighbour Alford on the main road. It seems that Alford
enjoyed a reputation for its mineral waters – they were
described as a quick purger good for all sharp humours or
obstruction. But sad to say, even by the late 1600s the place
was losing status, not because of the waters but for the lack
of decent accommodation, the locals being said to be 'a
clownish rude people'. In 1800 they were still struggling on,
for here, it was said, was a mineral water of the same kind
as that of Epsom in Surrey. But there must have been some
connexion – against all the recommended benefits of such
aperients – between the taking of the water and the ill-
humour of the inhabitants. For by 1830 all mention of the
waters has ceased, and what was then said of the place? 'The
society to be found at Castle Cary is so respectable, that
it is deservedly considered as a place of very agreeable retirement.'

The Ogilby route finally found its way to Bridgwater and
Barnstaple by aiming north of Somerton and Taunton and
struggling over the Polden Hills. The turnpikes developed
the way through Somerton and Langport and Taunton. The
new turnpike road that became the A303 continued south
through Ilchester and Ilminster to Honiton. And here, as
many have felt, arises the almost mythical barrier of the
Fosseway that divides the earliest English peoples from all
the others who followed on. To west of it lay Avalon and
the Isle of the Blest that received Arthur (and Alfred too)
when they were weary and must renew their strength. Much
of it is marsh, and, with its holy isle of Glastonbury, akin
to Hereward's fens with their Isle of Ely. Certainly it was
a land of secret ways – Merlin's ways.

BRISTOL TO WEYMOUTH

Inevitably, in a review of this nature, there must be a tendency towards the main throughways, or the work would never come to an end. Nevertheless a quick look at one of the minor roads is justifiable, since it will typify the thousands of miles of them that must have existed in these isles from earliest times. Many of these are due to the fact that in Wessex there were useful landing-places wherever there was coastline; but the coast was of such irregular shape that, as with the rivers, it was often worthwhile trying to find a short cut overland, rather than take the more simple course of water travel.

An example of what, in Ogilby's 1675 survey, was a principal cross road, was that from Bristol to Weymouth, from the outer fringes of Wessex deep into its heart. Bristol was one of England's premier cities from early medieval days, and the Gough map of 1360, besides showing roads from it to London and the Midlands, has traces of others running south. In the course of time the urban nature of the place was so marked that its main roads were barred to heavy wheeled traffic and transport was by sledge or dog-cart. A visitor at the end of the 1700s was writing 'with its hackney coaches, crowded streets, busy faces, smoke and noise, one could easily imagine oneself in the Strand'.

Weymouth is almost due south of Bristol, and the normal route today is by Shepton Mallet, Castle Cary or Wincanton, Sherborne and Dorchester, a distance of some seventy miles. Ogilby took an utterly different route which by his actual road measurements came to seventy-four miles, exactly the same figure as that given by a modern map measurer tracing his course on a modern map. This is all but uncanny. Ogilby made great claims for his methods of measurement, using the present mileage standard, against all previous methods by computation. His 'dimensurator' was a modern map measurer on a big scale, a large hand-propelled wheel incorporating a measuring device read by

the surveyor or his assistant. This random check confirms
that Ogilby was highly alert to what he was doing and which
route he selected. In this instance he frankly stated that the
road was in great part a bad, deep way, but maybe it offered
better accommodation.

The route kept west of the north–south line from Bristol
to Weymouth. It ran to Wells, Glastonbury, Somerton,
Crewkerne, then south-east along today's A356 through
Maiden Newton, whence at Frampton it cut south (avoiding Dorchester) to Upwey, near Weymouth. In detail, this
meant a singularly direct run to Wells, cutting down from
Bedminster to West Harptree (Hartry as Ogilby had it) and
over the Mendips (the lead mines, he wrote). Leaving Wells,
with the inevitable gallows perched outside the town, the
road ran to Glastonbury, then to Street, and continued southwards through Compton and Dundon to Somerton – a large
but poor town, said Ogilby. On he went through Longload
to Martock and ever southwards to Crewkerne.

To do so his route had to pass the Fosseway, which at
this point coincides with the modern A303, and it is interesting to remember that this same A303 did not seem to lead
in his day southwards to Ilminster and Exeter, but only to
Taunton and Barnstaple. The evidence given by this Ogilby
route is similar. It had to cross the Fosseway and, exactly
as happens today, it made a short journey along it before
branching down to Crewkerne. But there was no suggestion
of its being a main road crossing; there was just a direction,
on the one hand to Ilchester and on the other to Petherton
bridge. This again agrees with Stukeley's description in
1723. Ilchester and the Fosse were of no account and
he only noted that for a short distance the Roman quarry-
stone paving of the Fosse was intact. His sketch gave no
contemporary destinations for the Roman road, as though
it were out of use.

So far the way has been plain enough, but from South
Perrott, entering Dorset, it ascended the downs by Win-
nians Gap and its course is clear on Taylor's map of the
mid-1700s, past the Warr stone to the Corscombe turning

by the Hoarstone, which was also shown by Ogilby. It ran along Taylor's 'Ridge' over Rampisham Down and so to Maiden Newton. It reached Frampton on the Frome, one of those typical sites by the old Roman hard-core road from Dorchester to Ilchester on which the Normans had established a monastery. It was an alien one, sending its profits abroad, and did not long survive. Towards the end of the 1700s a Roman mosaic was found at Frampton that was said to bear indications of a definite Christian emblem. If, as so many maintain, Christianity did in fact reach Britain in Roman times through the West Country tin trade and remained centred in Glastonbury, Frampton would be a natural place for a missionary to reach, along this same Roman road that led all the way to Glastonbury.

The road by which Ogilby travelled through Dorset was not the Saxon village route along the river valleys, but the upland-route, so frequently preferred in this country; it was of undoubted remote origin and has continued in use down to the present day, when a number of these high-level roads have been brought up to modern motoring standards. As regards the Roman Yeovil–Ilchester road, it seems to have become neglected till revived as a turnpike, though it was certainly the shorter way to Somerton on the Bristol–Weymouth route.

At Frampton the road ignored Dorchester and cut across country. At the end of Frampton, said Ogilby, you crossed the Frome and went up a hill, which from Taylor's map was not the lower crossing at Muckleford but the one quoted as an alternative by R. Good in his *Old Roads of Dorset*: 'By the old road to the lodge at point 426'. Taylor showed that the rest of Ogilby's route was still in use a hundred years later, by Winterborne Steepleton over Blackdown Hill, with the alternate ways on Friar Waddon Hill across the Ridgeway and so to the Dorchester road at Broadwey.

There remains an overriding question: for what purpose should there be communication between Bristol and Weymouth? Enough to require an 'indifferent, well-frequented road'. ('Indifferent' was used by Ogilby in the sense of 'average', as with 'good, bad or indifferent'). He did not suggest that the road carried much trade, but it was sufficiently justified as leading from the Atlantic, which he called the North Sea, to the Channel, which he called the South. The need must have been a maritime one. Was it to collect knitted goods for the Merchant Navy or the Americas, and distribute sugar and specialized marine gear? Weymouth was an active importer of Spanish and Portuguese wines. How far were they sent inland to rival the Bristol imports?

Was its cross-country route from Frampton to Weymouth just a memory of that little alien monastery which had its visiting prelates from Normandy and sent its produce thither? Oddly enough, there was another of these alien establishments not far away at Loders. Perhaps the prelates worked in unison on their visits – they were not over-popular and would have felt safer in company, avoiding the perils and temptations of Dorchester. A later change in Church administration, from 1542 to 1836, saw the county of Dorset transferred from the see of Salisbury to that of Bristol. But that was not a period when the needs of bishops demanded special road networks.

CHAPTER SEVEN

Dorset and its Frontiers

THE LONDON–WEYMOUTH ROAD

IN his survey of 1675, John Ogilby set out to link every seaport – every mile of the coast, it would seem – with London. Weymouth at that time was an essential choice; in his own words it 'had very small beginning till of late it is arrived to a greater splendour and enjoys an indifferent good trade to France, Newfoundland etc'. Fifty years on, and even before George III made its name as a fashionable bathing resort, Defoe was to find it 'a sweet, clean, agreeable town, well-built, with many substantial merchants in it.' As for Dorchester, the county town, both Ogilby and Miss Fiennes shortly after, paid tribute to its fair, wide streets, its spacious market place and its manifold other blessings.

With all these attractions at the end of the journey, it is extraordinary that Ogilby's route from London, which took him from Basingstoke to Stockbridge and remote places like Broughton and Downton, should seem so archaic. There was nothing to prevent his recommending the well-used Land's End road through Andover and the sophisticated delights of Salisbury. His proposals may have been more direct on paper, though he got so lost in Cranborne Chase that any economy in mileage would have been thrown away. It should be added that no actual record has been found of anybody who followed the whole of the route as a throughway from London to Dorchester; but it was copied by many map-makers of the 1700s who continued to show it as a coach road until the turnpikes were made, varying the doubtful parts according to their fancy.

It is all this that makes the Ogilby route of such unusual interest. Its central part between Stockbridge and Blandford must represent some early medieval route, and much of it, except for purely local purposes, must have all but gone out of use when he included it. South-east Dorset was cut off from metropolitan England by a belt of forest – the New Forest and Cranborne Chase. When the king's influence was active in those famous hunting-grounds, a passage through them would not be sought by anybody unless he was on royal business; a trader who found his stocks depleted by the king's servants would have little hope of compensation. And until the turnpike opened them up to Georgian pleasure travellers there can have been little first-hand knowledge of the roads, such as they were, in those exclusive areas.

As late as 1752, for example, the *Gentleman's Magazine* was complaining that 'all beyond Sarum, or Dorchester, is to us terra incognita'; which was certainly at variance with Ogilby's claim, seventy-five years previously, that his Weymouth route 'afforded in general a good and well beaten road, and everywhere replenished with fitting entertainment to accommodate travellers'. But nobody would take exception to the first part of his route, that from London to Basingstoke, which was the same as the Land's End road that branched off from Basingstoke to Andover and Salisbury. From Basingstoke it pursued a course that appears in no other Ogilby description, and maybe it was surveyed by a rather below-par assistant who was more concerned to finish the job and put his feet up than to make an accurate record of where he had been.

At any rate, from Basingstoke the road ran an 'indirect and partly woody' course towards Popham Lane, very much as the Stockbridge road does today. It is surprising how often this corner of Hampshire appears in these studies of the Wessex road network. Passing motorists, to whom the name Popham Lane means nothing, cannot have an inkling of how well known it was to Georgian and Victorian West Country travellers. A century after Ogilby's survey

there was a tollgate there – the Oxdown gate they called it
– separating the takings on the Winchester turnpike from
those on the Stockbridge–Salisbury one. Everybody
stopped there for another excellent reason, the Wheatsheaf Inn and Posting House – that same Wheatsheaf which
will be found today performing very much the same sort of
function. If present intentions are carried through, the
motoring world will shortly become familiar enough with
the name of Popham Lane. It appears as the projected terminus of the new London motorway, the M3, which will
cross the Thames near Chertsey.

Even before the turnpikes were built it was an important
landmark on the crossroads of the Alresford–North Waltham–Overton road with the Micheldever–Winchester and
Stockbridge routes. There is something very, very old about
this crossroads. Any old map that shows the 'Hundred'
divisions will give one of these boundary lines running along
the Basingstoke road to Wheatsheaf Cross – and this is the
line of the old Roman road – till it reached the crossroads.
Here one of the hundred boundaries turned west along the
line of the Stockbridge road but just north, perhaps the
early trackway to Popham Beacon. The other boundary
swung directly south, past Breach Farm, to that neglected
and unexcavated Roman site between Woodmancott and
Chilton Candover named Stanchester. Here it turned very
firmly south-east as though, when the boundary was fixed,
it were following the definite line of a road that led to and
around Stanchester, which must have been an actual above-
ground site. There is evidence that parts of it were visible
within the last 200 years, and it is always surprising that nobody has associated it with the lost Antonine station of Vin-
domis.

The Wheatsheaf Inn will have known many an illustri-
ous visitor, but is unlikely to have had another chance of
an encounter such as might have occurred in the latter part
of the 1700s when it served as a dining headquarters for the
Hampshire Hunt. Mr Vernon, the then proprietor, no
doubt kept a watchful eye for a call from a particularly grand

member of the hunt, HRH Prinny, the future George IV, who had a house close at hand which was graced by his Hampshire friend Mrs Fitzherbert. Mr Vernon was probably far too busy on these duties of State to notice the casual visits of a rather graceless young lady, meeting the coach or collecting the mail. That was a pity, because the young lady, from Steventon up the lane, was Parson Austen's daughter, Miss Jane.

From Popham Lane the Weymouth road forked right towards Sutton Scotney, though it may have kept rather closer to the Micheldever valley than at present. It made its way to Stockbridge, which, said Ogilby, afforded 'very good accommodation to travellers: enjoying formerly a market which is now disused'. The problem of the road here presents itself. The market town, founded about 1200, had by the 1600s failed to make the grade. Winchester and Weyhill would no doubt have dealt with major needs, and the local population or trade had become insufficient to justify the small weekly market.

As Ogilby made clear, Stockbridge was not then regarded as being on the main London road from the west. It stood on the road between Winchester and Southampton and Salisbury, both the Hampshire towns being at that time at the lowest ebb of their fortunes and unlikely to be attracting steady business, which would have passed to Salisbury; and it stood on this mysterious road to Dorset which again could not have been looked on as a money-spinner. Those who were intending to visit south-east Dorset would surely have selected the well-tested route through Andover and Salisbury, and thence through Cranborne to Blandford or Wimborne.

What made the Ogilby route seek this somewhat neglected township of Stockbridge and then, instead of continuing to Salisbury, plunge into the unknown as soon as it had crossed the Test, to Broughton, West Tytherley and West Dean on the Hampshire border, to Downton in Wiltshire and Cranborne in Dorset? Who were these travellers whose needs had produced, to quote Ogilby's unusual phrase, 'a good and well beaten road, everywhere with fitting entertainment'? Or was he even taking advice from his patron Charles II who would certainly have retained memories of Dorset's roads for the whole of his life?

The thought is not entirely fanciful. When Charles was on the run from Worcester he is known to have passed near the old palace of Clarendon and could well have heard of a short cut to London coming from Cranborne to Stockbridge. He would have been told that it was well known to his Norman ancestors, who did a lot of hunting round there in days gone by.

There is far worse to follow with this eccentric Weymouth road, but meanwhile the link-up as far as Downton might seem reasonable, at any rate for a horse traveller. Broughton, like Kings Somborne east of the Test, was a natural filter for traffic between Stockbridge and Romsey. 'A place of good accommodation,' wrote Ogilby. Just beyond it – a most pleasant road this today, though not so long ago it would have been wood or scrub land as far as Poole Harbour – the Ogilby road crossed that famous Roman way from Winchester to Old Sarum, which here is motorable in either direction.

The road ambled down through West Tytherley and West Dean, where the Hampshire/Wiltshire boundary goes through the village inn. Ogilby's surveyor was by this time so muddled that he called it East Dean, and it is to be regretted that he did not seek guidance from the young Miss Fiennes (born in 1662), whose mother – and it was she who inspired the travel itch in her daughter – came from these parts (Normans Court, West Tytherley). She could have listed the local landowners, growing their 'groves of Scott and Norroway firrs in rows all in sight of the road'; and she certainly knew that the London road ran back to Stockbridge and Sutton Scotney. She might even, despite her ultra-Roundhead parentage, have put the surveyor on a reasonable route to Blandford.

At West Dean the road met that way along the Lockerley valley which the Winchester bishops must surely have used on journeys to their property of Downton. It took the southerly course – the one towards West Grimstead – and motorists will lose it here as they must turn left up the hill to Whiteparish. But the Ogilby way continued from West Dean along the foot of the ridge till it reached a point marked 280 ft on the 1-inch Ordnance maps for Salisbury or the New Forest, where a track or lane comes in from East Grimstead.

Here on the left are two tracks climbing up the hillside at an angle, and since this is now National Trust land, it is used at the foot as a car park while the passengers make the right-hand trek up to the Pepperbox. The Ogilby road would, however, be the left-hand one, indicated by a kink in his chart, which would take him away from what in his time would have been private ground belonging to Brick-worth House. The Pepperbox, or Summerhouse as it was called, presumably before pepperboxes were common enough for their shapes to become nicknames, came later.

The Ogilby road thus emerged at the west end of White-parish, at what later became a tollgate, crossing both the Romsey A27 and the Southampton A36. This A36 must have developed as the early Norman link between the royal homes at Clarendon, Lyndhurst and Beaulieu, via Bram-shaw and Minstead. The connexions with Southampton and Romsey (A27) can only have come later, after the founding of Salisbury. It is indeed quite likely that the Ogil-by route at this stage is the most venerable of the three, being in the line of succession from the pre-Roman ridge-way from Winchester to the Avon at Charford. It can be followed down the small lane on the left at the west end of Whiteparish beyond the crossroads; then across the A36.

Here again, where Ogilby's surveyor plunged into 'ye forest', there still remains a strong feeling of antiquity and it is not difficult to see the princeling Cerdic, fresh from his victory over the Roman-British at Charford in 519, approaching Winchester to claim the kingdom of Wessex. But so far as the surveyor was concerned, he must have been glad to descend the great hill to Downton and write up his notes. They were depressing enough, just a record of Downton's past glories, the Saxons and the Normans and the once lively market that was dwindling to nothing. In one respect it was even worse than Stockbridge – there was never a word in his report about 'fitting accommodation'.

It is strange that the two market towns which have been met on the day's run, Stockbridge and Downton, were both deliberately encouraged and expanded about 1200. Both were facing hard times, though the sheep industry was booming. Stockbridge, perhaps, was becoming too much dependent on transit trade; Downton had become an out-of-the-way place once it lost the link with the Winchester bishops.

At Downton, where the Ogilby road crossed the River Avon, the boundaries of three counties came together in a most curious manner. Just south of the townlet, which is in Wiltshire, Hampshire juts into Wiltshire and Dorset so as to possess the old Avon crossing at Charford and protect it by the hill fort of Whitsbury above Rockbourne. This is not entirely fanciful, for it can be seen how these ancient county boundaries follow the Grims Ditches and Bokerley Dyke, which can safely be said to be pre-Norman.

CRANBORNE CHASE

Also to be considered is Cranborne Chase, of which the outer bounds overran the three county boundaries and covered the whole area west of the Avon from Ringwood to Salisbury. All this country, like the New Forest east of the Avon, was subject to very strict control in medieval times and would not be popular with travellers, though the inner chase – which really was taboo – would not affect their passage as it lay more to the westward. Within this borderland there are perhaps as many traces of man's history throughout the ages as anywhere in the world.

In order to see what lay behind the Ogilby road, that was so soon to vanish as a constituent whole, it is necessary to have a quick look at east Dorset as it emerged in earlier days. East Dorset for this purpose must be taken to include a good slice of modern Hampshire; as recently as Tudor times the county boundary was held to run along the Avon to Christchurch, and Bournemouth Chine, or Durley Chine a few hundred yards west of it, was taken for it into Victoria's reign. East Dorset extends to Dorchester. The incoherent hill patterns west of the county town are the frontiers of another land.

The flat, well-watered eastern side of the county always found favour with the ruling classes of successful invaders – places like Corfe and Wareham, Canford and Cranborne. How did medieval communications run, first with Winchester, and later with London? How could they run, when the whole area from Southampton Water to the River Stour that flows thorugh Blandford and Wimborne to Christchurch was a royal hunting preserve? Till well into Norman times they must have relied on the existing Celtic-Roman network, which was mainly a linking up of fortified Iron Age townships with some trading additions; to which there would be later developments brought about by the need of royalty to move from one sporting residence to another.

The hard core of this system would have been the major Roman road from London to Silchester, Old Sarum, and Badbury Rings near Wimborne, with branches thence to Poole Harbour and Dorchester. General experience in Wessex shows that this type of road remained in use for all of 1,000 years, up to the 1300–1400s. What is curious is that in south-east Dorset the system seems to have been discarded at a much earlier date, for the two Roman crossings of the Stour were soon replaced by alternative Norman sites. It may be that the big engineering project, which had carried the Roman road across the marshy Frome east of Dorchester, had failed from lack of maintenance, and another entrance to the town, from the north, was brought into use until the old route was remade in the 1700s. This would have led to the growth of towns such as Milton Abbas and Blandford, north of the original line.

The other Roman way from London, by Silchester and

Winchester and then through Nursling, Cadnam, Stoney Cross to Poole Harbour, was probably a minor route concerned with trade, but it seems clear that it has always been kept in being, even though its exact course west of Stoney Cross remains undefined till there is a trace of it near Canford where it joined the road from Badbury.

It would be impossible to make much progress in reconstructing these old throughways were it not for the large-scale country maps which appeared in the 1700s when people were starting to tour for pleasure along the new turnpikes, but which naturally showed the earlier roads that have since vanished. Roads admit no boundaries, and the debt hereabouts is threefold, to Isaac Taylor for his *Hampshire* (1759) and *Dorset* (1765), and Andrews and Dury for their *Wiltshire* (1773). Taylor was an ardent antiquarian within the limits of his age, and his Roman roads were drawn so definitely that they give the impression of being not only visible but in actual use. And since most of those he shows are accurate enough, it would be foolish to ignore the few which do not appear on our present maps.

For example, the route of the Roman road from Badbury to Hamworthy on Poole Harbour, passing just west of Wimborne and through Upton, is nowadays well established, though the evidence at the Badbury end is sketchy. Taylor's alternative was perhaps projected straight back from the visible stretch at Upton, but it made him bypass Badbury and join the main Old Sarum road north of it near Witchampton. Here he shows twin roads setting out almost parallel to each other, as though one might have been aiming for Badbury but just petered out. The map may have been known to Sir R. Colt Hoare, the Wiltshire antiquary, who some fifty years later recorded signs of a Roman way leaving the main Icknield Street southward at Manswood, exactly the same point. There is a modern school of thought, which may not have depended on Taylor's map, that considers the Roman road from London to have in the first place been aiming for Hamworthy, and only included Dorchester afterwards.

The pull of Poole Harbour has always been considerable, if not always appreciated. It shifted from Roman Hamworthy to Saxon Wareham, finally to Norman Poole. Wareham had been badly mauled by the Danes and this may have left a gap in the harbour's activities, though it must certainly have remained the premier site in the harbour till towards the end of the 1100s, despite further pillaging in the disturbances of Stephen's unhappy reign. The importance attached to Corfe Castle by John in the early 1200s suggests that Wareham's prestige continued till then, but it cannot have been much later when Poole took over. The minute hamlet of Poole did not start to take shape till well after the Conquest, perhaps about 1160, and then only because it formed part of – and was the closest point on the harbour to – the powerful manor of Canford, near Wimborne.

From earliest times there have been recognized land routes which followed the line of the coasts, and it would have been natural to find some form of track from Christchurch across to Poole, Wareham and the Purbecks to Weymouth. Yet as comparatively lately as the 1500s Leland could only record that the way between Wareham and Poole was low and moorish; to avoid it there was even a ferry from the inlet of Lytchett Bay across to Poole. And Poole was so recently expanded, he said, that there were men still living who had known almost the whole place when it was covered with sedge and rushes.

Till last century, to reach Dorchester from the east the traveller must needs journey round by Wareham. There was no direct road from Christchurch across the heath. It sounds fantastic, but the present road from Poole to Bere Regis, the A35, was only completed in 1841, contemporary with the growth of Bournemouth. Not till then did the one-time capital of Wessex, Winchester, possess a direct link with its south-western territories!

The governing medieval factor in this no-man's-land was Canford, that same Canford which produced the first Earl of Salisbury, whose family's monuments are so honoured among the treasures of Salisbury Cathedral.

Without question this rather stupid lack of east–west contact, in contrast with an ample north–south communication, was mainly due to the episcopal sees of Winchester and Salisbury following the approximate county boundary between Hampshire and Dorset along the Avon. And thus it was that, though for centuries the trunk road from London to Poole had been that through Winchester and Ringwood, the alternative through Salisbury was always a strong competitor. It is a pretty quirk of history that the traffic centre of this Salisbury route should become Cranborne, from which in the 1800s emerged that L. D. G. Tregonwell whose name, long known in Dorset, became woven into the first records of modern Bournemouth.

What seems to have happened to the Roman road system is that the Badbury–Dorchester road failed with the breakdown of the Frome Causeway; that the Badbury–Poole Harbour road failed when the site of Poole (via Canford) was preferred to Hamworthy; and that the Winchester–Ringwood–Poole Harbour road, finding its Dorset end for a long period out of use, became diverted from Ringwood to Canford, Wimborne and the Stour. Badbury became neglected as a road centre in favour of Cranborne, and even today it is clear how Saxon and Norman sites like Corfe and Wareham, Bindon Abbey and the great nunnery at Tarrant Rushton were linked to Cranborne by the two Norman crossings of the Stour at Sturminster Marshall and Spettisbury. The growth of Blandford higher up the river was probably later – the first mention of it as a borough was in 1307 – and was possibly due to its offering a level surface on both sides of the river and thus providing a useful stopping-place on the ways to Dorchester and Shaftesbury.

This preference of a road to Old and then New Sarum instead of one to Winchester, maybe of Cranborne Chase instead of the New Forest, is most marked in the case of that restless, hunt-loving monarch John, in the early 1200s. Frequently in the Chase, his journeys to it from London or Windsor never seemed to take him through Winchester. He chose other old Roman routes, by Freemantle near Basing-stoke, Ludgershall or Marlborough. At the end of the 1200s Edward I, who spent much time in the New Forest, was seldom recorded as being in Winchester. Often he visited religious houses on the Stour and the Frome, often he travelled between Canford and Ringwood and Lynd-hurst; back he would go to Clarendon on the outskirts of Salisbury.

It was during this century that the new cathedral city of Salisbury was being founded, with its new bridge that was to ruin the old Wiltshire capital of Wilton. The road from east Dorset back through Cranborne was established – a royal highway, a monastic highway. Apart from Ringwood, the main crossing of the Avon for a trader who, for example, was concerned with the export of wools from the Solent ports, was at Fordingbridge.

North of Fordingbridge came the bridge at Downton, that Wiltshire township which remained the property of the Win-chester bishops and in these same 1200s was actively de-veloped by them. It was in Downton, before this brief digression on east Dorset, that the study of the Ogilby route of 1675 from London to Dorchester and Weymouth was suspended.

This book is concerned to retrace throughways that did exist, not fantasies. The Ogilby route between Downton and Blandford is valuable, not for what it shows but for what it should have shown. A glance at the modern map will reveal that without much divergence a straight line between Downton and Cranborne will pass the Avon crossing at Charford, the Saxon church at Breamore, the vast Roman villa site on the outskirts of Rockbourne and go on through Damerham. This is the type of route suggested by the small-scale maps of the 1700s, which were obviously using a route of extreme antiquity that they could recognize, in-stead of the two-sides-of-the-triangle diversions of Ogilby.

His route ran due west across the downs from the Down-ton suburb of Wick to join the Salisbury–Cranborne road between Toyd Farm and Tidpit. It can still be followed as a track, or it can be met by taking the modern made-up road from Rockbourne to the junction of Toyd Farm, which cuts across it just south-west of Duck's Nest. At Toyd Farm it met the old Saxon way from Wilton, and it is easy to guess that this was the route that would have been used by the staff of the Winchester bishops passing from their Downton to their Hindon possessions. It would be the shortest way to avoid complications either with their brothers of Sarum or with the royal owners of the Chase; it avoided villages.

From Cranborne the same direct route that ran from Charford on the Avon continued across the downs to Spettisbury on the Stour, and much of it is in evidence today. In fact, were it not for enclosures at St Giles and Crichel and the airfield at Tarrant Rushton, it might all be in evidence. The St Giles bulge is encountered soon after leaving Cranborne on the Wimborne road B3078; Taylor's map of the mid-1700s showed the pre-enclosure picture with the road going straight through the park (note the tumuli). Taylor also recorded that the point was known as Coldharbour where, as is so clear today, the old road emerges from the park at the lodge gates just east of Knowlton. The nearby cottages are still known as Coldharbour. They seem too far away from the hard Roman Badbury road to have obtained the name from there, and it seems to have arisen to denote the junction of the Wimborne road with the old Iron Age route between Whitsbury and Spettisbury.

The road continued past (or through) the ancient circle at Knowlton and crossed the Allen at Stanbridge, where an oldish bridge near the Horton Inn records its passage. Oddly enough, a map attributed to the early 1600s and showing the boundaries of the Chase, suggested that the boundary followed the road along this stretch from the (later) lodge gates of St Giles, passing through Knowlton and bending round to Stanbridge, whence it accompanied the Allen downstream. It names 'Peters Bridge' crossing a little tributary, prior to the artificial lake, running up to Moor Crichel. The road continued its course by the abbey house at Witchampton, through the village over the barrow-studded downs north of Badbury to the Stour at Crawford, leading to Spettisbury.

In Ogilby's day there would have been no apparent difficulty in taking this straightforward route, branching off for Tarrant Monkton and Blandford at Stanbridge. But his surveyor took such an impossible course that it is a waste of time trying to pursue it. There is only one check that can be placed upon it, that of the two points where his map coincides with the map of his Salisbury–Cranborne–Wimborne road, which seems to have been covered by another, more reliable surveyor. At the first checkpoint, where the Weymouth road from Downton is said to have joined the Salisbury road between Toyd Farm and Tidpit, the second surveyor made no mention of a link with Downton. But immediately after Cranborne he did show a sign to Blandford on the right, which is the way the debatable first surveyor tried to go. All that can be said with confidence (and other maps from the 1700s agree with this) is that the route did reach Tarrant Monkton, perhaps passing College Farm at Gussage All Saints, and entered Blandford by the racecourse, which is now the Army camp.

R. Good, in the second edition of his *Old Roads of Dorset*, suggests an interpretation which is not really related to Ogilby's road; this latter might have run parallel to the Gussage stream without crossing it, and then seemed to get so close to Chettle that it might as well have continued to Blandford through the pre-turnpike Pimperne road.

Stukeley, in his 1723 tour, followed the Roman way from Old Sarum and reached Woodyates where 'it then becomes the common road for half a mile, but immediately passes forward upon a down, the road going off to the right'. Thus it emerges that the present A354 takes the same line as its pre-turnpike predecessor. He continued along the 'Icklingdike' and

descended a valley where a brook crosses it, from two villages called Glisset. At All-Saints, or Lower Glisset, there was a small alehouse, and the only one hereabouts

(the Rose); my old landlady, after some discourse pre-
paratory, informed me that at Boroston, a mile lower
upon the river, had been an old city ... that ruins and
foundations were there ... that many old coins had
been ploughed up when she was a girl, which the children commonly played withall ... This place being not
capable of affording me a proper mansion, I left the more
particular scrutiny of it for another opportunity. Hence
I pursued the road on the opposite chalk hill, where they
now have dug it away to burn for lime, but much degenerate from Roman mortar in strength: it was not
long before I absolutely lost it in great woods beyond
Long Crechil; but by information I learnt that it passes
the Stour at Crayford bridge below Blandford, where I
was obliged to take up my nightly quarters.

Boroston (Bowerswain today) is now a farm site, but it
is notable how many old maps took their Cranborne–
Blandford route along by it, and a visit there can still con-
vey the one-time importance of the place. The origin of the
tale of past grandeur that so affected the landlady of the
Rose Inn has never, it would seem, been probed. Even the
Rose Inn is gone without trace. But Stukeley's departure
from the Roman road is significant. It remains lost at the
point where he lost it (in the chalk pit). He could have
picked it up shortly afterwards, but he followed local
opinion which obviously preferred the 'Coldharbour'
route just described from Charford to Crawford, which also
ran close to Bowerswain and which crossed the Roman
road just after the latter vanished, between Whitchampton
and Hemsworth.

Now having, in some fashion or other, reached Blandford and a much-needed rest – and what a relief to find the
Ogilby opinion that it was 'a place affording no mean entertainment to travellers' – it will be useful once again to
take stock. A glance at the map makes it clear that the way
to Dorchester and Weymouth is following an angular
course in contrast to that to other coastal points. South of

Blandford lies Bere Regis, with a road running almost straight down to the sea at Lulworth through Bindon Abbey and Wool. It is tempting to speculate whether this road was started by invaders following the ridgeway inland, or by natives attracted to the Lulworth lobsters. Bere Regis is also united with Poole Harbour by the early (Coldharbour) road from Wareham. But of course it was not Bere Regis that was the magnet (the Regis came from a huntingbox of John's about 1201), but the Iron Age Woodbury Hill that was to become the centre of the great Wessex fair.

Up to the mid-1800s there was no main road eastwards from Bere to Poole, and the route from Dorchester that reached Bere ran to Wimborne. Miss Fiennes, about 1698, recorded travelling *over* Woodbury Hill, 'eminent for a great Fair'. She did not mention Bere. It was as though that was still the normal route. Thus one way and another there is considerable evidence to support the conclusion that the contact between east Dorset and the New Forest was very small. Reference has already been made to the travels of King John in the opening 1200s. Often in Dorset, he covered the area bounded eastwards by Cranborne and Bere to the Purbecks. Only once was he noted on a visit to Canford, twice to Christchurch; to Ringwood or Poole not at all.

At the end of the 1200s Edward I, who again gave ample evidence that many of the Roman hardways were still in active use, did once proceed from Bindon, near Wool, to Canford, and so, no doubt by Ringwood, to Nursling and Winchester. Ringwood he used frequently, though only in conjunction with his journeys along the Stour, and almost always on his circular tours that led him to Lyndhurst and back to Clarendon, which was his obvious preference to Winchester as a headquarters.

In the 1500s there is the same picture. Leland travelled the coastal Dorset route, reaching Poole from the west. Thence he travelled through Wimborne to Cranborne and Salisbury, making no mention of Downton except to record that it had a stone bridge. He also visited Christ-

church, but from the New Forest. He noted the road between it and Poole, though it was clear that he never made
the journey, but remained in Hampshire. It was only a few
years later that the alum and copperas workings were being started up along the coast at Bournemouth and in Poole
Harbour, financed by the lord of Canford. This would
have helped to open up the route along the coast.

And so to Ogilby's own time, the late 1600s, with Celia
Fiennes, who was often in these parts, even travelling to
Brownsea Island in Poole Harbour to see the copperas
workings – and eat the lobsters. But she came from, and returned to, Wimborne and the west. She never seems to have
visited either Christchurch or Ringwood, and thought that
the Avon divided the New Forest from Wiltshire. She gave
no indication of a main road even in Cranborne Chase. She
crossed it from Wilton to Blandford 'through a hare warren and a forest of the kings'; and she rode from Blandford to Salisbury – 'I came to a gate which brought me into
Wiltshire and so over to the downs'.

About the only record of consequence where the 'official'
road from Poole to London via Winchester was used comes
in that tale of the captured Duke of Monmouth after his
stupid, vain-glorious rising. He was captured in 1685, within ten years of Ogilby's first edition, between Wimborne
and Cranborne and in theory should certainly have been
led to the Tower through Downton or at least Salisbury.
In fact he was taken immediately to Ringwood and then
heavily escorted through the New Forest and Winchester,
all the way round by Guildford. It seems that Ogilby's mystery road through Downton was unrecognized in the neighbourhood, which relied on the garrisoned route. But his
survey of this London–Winchester–Ringwood–Poole route
only supported its lack of contact with the country to the
west. From the New Forest to Poole he gave no side road
direction to Dorchester or even Wareham. From Poole itself the only other route shown led to Salisbury; between
Ringwood and Poole the only side directions were to Wimborne and Cranborne.

Defoe, slightly later, travelled the coast like his predecessors. He did make the journey from Christchurch to Poole, which was growing fast with its trade to Newfoundland, but to do so rode via Wimborne. The country between Wimborne and Poole was 'sandy wild and barren'. This was the same country, the outskirts of Bere Heath, that had such a macabre fascination for Hardy, and indeed for anybody else till in recent years it has become a more material nightmare land of great roads and military machines and atomic factories.

It all points to a determination in east Dorset to avoid the see of Winchester and its minor possession at Downton; to aim for Cranborne and the see of Salisbury; to maintain contact with the west. The roads made their great memorials with their bridges at Crawford, Wimborne and Sturminster Marshall, where the Whitemill crossing would have led to Hinton Parva and the Horton–Cranborne road that was probably the first route from Wimborne. It was not till the latter half of the 1700s that the country really became accessible with the making of the turnpike from Salisbury to Blandford; it bypassed the old village way (Tarrant Hinton and Gussage St Andrew) that marked the bounds of the inner furtiveness of Cranborne Chase.

BLANDFORD TO DORCHESTER

With these reflections the comforts of Blandford must be exchanged for those of Dorchester. As regards the latter, with its strange Shangri-La remoteness, here is Defoe's impression from, it might be said, Queen Anne's time. Daniel (Moll Flanders) Defoe was not unaware of the facts of life, and he could only conclude that it was 'indeed a pleasant agreeable town to live in ... a man who coveted a retreat in this world might as agreeably spend his time there as in any town in England'. Neither would a man starve there. Remote it might be, but not poor. Within six miles of the town's circumference, he reckoned, there were 600,000 sheep grazing.

It is odd that there is no trace of a hard Roman highway to Dorchester from Poole Harbour (either Hamworthy or Wareham). Their choice must have been the old ridgeway between the Frome and the Piddle that runs from Wareham to Tincleton, within easy reach of the hard road to Dorchester from Badbury. Trade to Hamworthy from the west presumably did not warrant a more direct route. As soon as the Roman causeway to Dorchester collapsed, the eastern route must have taken to the Saxon way, which was tenuous enough, represented today by that delightful route through Frome water meadows, with the great heath isolating it from the rest of the world; the route that runs through West Stafford, Woodsford, Moreton and East Burton to Wool and Bindon, the Holmes, Stoborough and Wareham. This was the way known to the Norman kings; the use of the present Winfrith route as the main one would have come later. Stukeley's sketch of Dorchester in 1723 confirmed the Poole road as proceeding via Wareham.

Westwards towards Bridport, communications were not so bright either. Miss Fiennes, about 1700, recorded that from Dorchester 'the ways are stony and very narrow'. This is nearer the truth than the quotations often attributed to Defoe at about the same period, which suggest a more sophisticated network. The original Defoe had nothing on the subject: he was badly handled in later editions which added material that could not have applied in his time, eg, references to 'turnpike gates' when he was writing in an age before the turnpike roads were made, and the description of the building of the new bridge at Dorchester in 1746, fifteen years after he was dead.

Northwards there was a fairly straightforward road to Sherborne, and a link between the county town and the once great religious centre of Shaftesbury.

Wimborne, as has been seen, was accessible from Dorchester through Bere Regis. If anything, the way was shorter than now, with less enclosed park to circumvent at Charborough. Miss Fiennes had no difficulty in reaching her relation Mr Erle at Charborough from Dorchester, crossing over Woodbury Hill. 'The road,' she said, 'passed by Charborough.' The great fairground at Woodbury would have made a strong road network essential.

Till the later 1700s, therefore, the main throughway approach to Dorchester and Weymouth must have come through Blandford, via the ecclesiastical link with Salisbury and the political link with London. The evidence that Ogilby's route from Downton to Cranborne and Blandford was ever a recognized main road is negligible. But before his final stretch between Blandford and Dorchester is studied, there are a few curious relics of the old crossings of the Stour that must be noted. They are all related to Taylor's map of 1765.

One of these is that his only reference to a Roman road at Badbury was the one to Hamworthy. He gave no hint of the extension from Badbury to the river at Shapwick for the Dorchester road, though such a track is suggested on the early Ordnance Survey drawings some forty years later. Neither map hints at the Bath road towards Tarrant Monkton. Taylor, without apparently knowing it, picked up the line of the Dorchester road some two miles west of the Stour, with a lane that formed the southern boundary of Coll Wood. The road appeared again east of Abbots Court by Winterborne Kingston and continued in use through Ashley Barn to Burleston, between Tolpuddle and Puddletown. Here it was merged into what is now the A35 joining these last two villages, and it can be assumed that its further extension to Stinsford and Dorchester passed out of service when the Frome causeway broke up.

But Taylor had more to show than this, a short distance along the Stour at that fine old bridge at Crawford, the crossing for Spettisbury. The modern map will show that a farm road runs either side of the Rings; the more northerly leading to South Farm and fading away at Combs Ditch, the more southerly stopping earlier. Taylor showed a much busier road network, with the two tracks uniting and taking a course over the northern end of Combs Ditch to meet the Blandford–Milborne road east of Winterborne Whitchurch.

There was also a second branch which led along the top
edge of Coll Wood and down across the southern end of
Combs Ditch to join the Roman road east of Abbots Court,
thus giving an alternative route to Dorchester. Excavations
at the Roman site west of Winterborne Kingston have
noted the tracks alongside the Roman way, and Margary in
his *Roman Roads in Britain* comments that, rather more
to the west, at Ashley Barn, there are holloways on either
side of the road.

Here again there is evidence from the remarkable journey of William Stukeley in 1723. It has already been traced
southwards to where he was assured that the Roman way
from Old Sarum crossed the Stour at Crawford Bridge by
Spettisbury encampment. (At that time Badbury was not
regarded as a major point: it is now located as the Roman
Vindogladia, which Stukeley took to be Bowerswain.) He
continued from Crawford and came, so it seems, to Combs
Ditch, 'another ditch and rampart', which he associated
with the Iron Age Belgae. Convinced that he was still pursuing the Roman road to Dorchester, he carried on to find
himself at Woodbury Hill, Bere Regis. 'By what I could
see or learn,' he wrote, 'in travelling over this intricate
country, the Roman road passes upon a division between
Pimpern and Bere Hundreds.' He had, without knowing it,
crossed the line of the real Roman road somewhere near
Winterborne Kingston, again mistaking, with local support,
a popular pre-Roman road for its successor. In Dorset it is
clear enough that the Celtic influence survived and out-
lasted the Roman.

Perhaps here lies an explanation of the utter lack of
some tradition outlining the route taken by the body of
Edward the Martyr from Wareham to Shaftesbury. He was
murdered by his stepmother in 978 at Corfe Castle. The
young king was interred at Wareham but some three years
later he was conveyed to greater sanctuary at Shaftesbury.
The route must have followed the Coldharbour way from
Wareham to Bere Regis, and then perhaps by this forgotten
Stukeley road that continued along the ridge to Shaftesbury

by Melbury Abbas. The reason why this notable route could have been forgotten is that most of it had disappeared from use. There is a curious confirmation for part of this route in an old tradition that the murderess, Elfrida, had by then gone to live at Bere and desired to take part in the funeral procession. But her horse resented her action and would only walk backwards.

It seems not unreasonable to associate these Spettisbury tracks with some form of network before the present road from Blandford to Dorchester came into use. The turnpike here was an early one (1756) and therefore appeared prominently on Taylor's map. It is generally agreed that Milton Abbas, slightly north of the turnpike, continued after the Reformation as a town of some status, till its slighting and rebuilding as a model village towards the end of the 1700s. The turnpike route, which bypassed it, must in fact have done considerable damage before the slighting, though the point has been overlooked by those who condemned the Lord Dorchester who settled its fate in 1786.

Now the Ogilby route (1675) to Dorchester, which has been faulted at every twist, ran from Blandford without touching any village except 'Milford' which can be assumed to be Milborne. It mentioned neither Winterborne Whitchurch nor the stream there, though in fairness the descriptive notes, with their details of turnings to avoid, make tolerable sense. That something equivalent to the modern way was open is made clear by Miss Fiennes, who at about the same date recorded a journey between Dorchester and Blandford which took her from Puddletown to Milborne and Whitchurch. The Ogilby road, however, took a recognizable course through Waterston, avoiding Puddletown, and at first glance might appear to be entering Dorchester by the present London road, although many local authorities have been satisfied that, until Greys Bridge and the rebuilt Roman causeway came into being some seventy years after Ogilby, this method of approach was only feasible in dry weather, and on the whole even dangerous. Anybody who enters Dorchester by the present London road and continues out of the town towards Weymouth, which was Ogilby's purpose, will make a roughly right-angled turn. The Ogilby route map suggested an almost straight way through the place, consistent with entering it by one of the more northerly routes. Such a route could proceed, as Taylor's map showed much later, to Waterston and Milton Abbas and Blandford. Ogilby's placing of Stinsford was completely in accord with this interpretation, which would be further helped by the location of another place-name that he gave, 'Stinsborrow'.

The old course of the eastern approach to Dorchester has been a source of doubt or controversy for so long that it seems strange for the Ogilby survey, which in the Dorset area has proved so questionable, to offer a feasible solution. It has been misinterpreted by those who took its entrance to the town as representing the present London road, whereas it only makes sense if the course of the river is seen to be the branch past Fordington, not the one under Greys Bridge. Fortunately Ogilby is fully supported by Stukeley with his sketch map of Dorchester dated August 22nd, 1723; in conjunction with Taylor's post-turnpike map an adequate picture emerges. The Blandford road ran due north from a point opposite Fordington church, crossing the Frome by a small bridge and proceeding by what Taylor called Slyers Lane east of Cokers Farm. Its course towards Waterston may still be marked by a footpath. A modern map still further confuses the issue by naming Slyers Lane as an east–west route to Stinsford. This was west of our B3143, but probably joined it once the river was past, and so made its way to Druce Farm and the present Blandford road beyond Puddletown. The two editions of Ronald Good's *Old Roads of Dorset* offer different interpretations, and it is uncertain whether his later (1966) view corresponds with this.

Viewed together these two pre-Greys Bridge sketches of Dorchester present a similar and unexpected story. The eastern end of the town is in effect bounded by this north–south road running between Fordington church and the

Pound west of it (Pound Lane). High East Street tended to ignore the present extension as London Road, but ran to Holloway Road and High Street, Fordington, whence, south of the church, was the only marked eastern exit 'to Pool'. To Stukeley the Icening Street bore no relation to the modern Icen Way, and followed the road beyond Fordington church, outside the walls, now called South Walks Road, to join the road from the west gate along the line of Damers Road. Parallel to High East and West Streets, and apparently of equal importance as throughways, was a road represented in part today by Durngate Street and Princes Street.

There is no need to follow the Ogilby route from Dorchester to Weymouth. It was straightforward, taking the only line across the ridgeway. A long, tortuous journey has been pursued from London. The value of the pursuit lies in its proof that, up to the mid-1700s when the turnpikes began to appear, south Dorset was all but isolated from the rest of England. There was no recognized means of reaching Dorchester, though most people would make their way to Salisbury and inquire the route as they went along. Otherwise they played safe and followed the coastline from wherever they first reached it. The characters brought out so strongly by Hardy were the direct creations of this shut-away Celtic-Roman-Saxon world, with its intense introspection and closeness to nature. The poet Barnes, with his more simple approach, felt it equally, and his views on the original English language probably deserve more study than they have received.

A short extract has already been given from the travelled, man-of-the-world Defoe when he met Dorchester society in this pre-turnpike era. Here is some more Defoe (authentic, not added later), which fully supports the findings of this study of the Dorset approaches ... On Dorchester,

Though here are divisions and the people are not all of one mind, either as to religion or politics, yet they did not seem to separate with so much animosity as in other places. Here I saw the Church of England clergyman and the Dissenting minister or preacher drinking tea together and conversing with civility and good neighbourhood, like Catholic Christians, and men of a catholic and extensive charity.

In contrast with society elsewhere

The Dorsetshire ladies are equal in beauty, and may be superior in reputation; in a word, their reputation seems here to be better kept; guarded by better conduct, and managed with more prudence, and yet the Dorsetshire ladies, I assure you, are not nuns, they do not go veiled about streets, or hide themselves when visited; but a general freedom of conversation, agreeable, mannerly, kind and good, runs through the whole body of the gentry of both sexes, mixed with the best of behaviour, and yet governed by prudence and modesty; such as I nowhere see better in all my observation, through the whole isle of Britain.

THE WESTERN ROAD FROM DORCHESTER

Somehow or other, after this arduous journey to Dorchester, a form of throughway must be found that will lead farther westwards. That means accepting the challenge of the western road towards Exeter, which has puzzled all antiquarians because of the trouble the Romans took to build up the Celtic route to their settlement of Eggardon, only to lose it as soon as it had got there. How, in effect, did one get to Bridport, let alone Exeter, in medieval days? There are at least five reasonable choices.

There was the coastal route, the pre-Roman ridgeway leading from the Purbecks across to the camp at Abbotsbury. This was the road followed in the first half of the 1500s by Leland, who travelled from Lyme to Bridport, avoided the contentious stretch to Dorchester by striking inland, but returned to Weymouth to follow the coast eastwards, The Bridport guide books miss the tale of how he was fooled there. They will relate that from time immemorial it has been one of England's chief centres for making rope, and they may add that a length of rope is known locally as a Bridport dagger. They omit to add that Leland dismissed the town by saying, 'Bridport is set as middle way betwixt Weymouth and Lyme. At Bridport be made good daggers.'

What is important is that he substituted Weymouth for Dorchester, and though he covered Dorset thoroughly he seems to have missed out the county town completely. But 100 years later, by the 1600s, the Dorchester–Bridport route was recognized by its inclusion in Ogilby's survey. Here again, it was only a minor road from the key town of Exeter, and when it reached Dorchester it confirmed previous conclusions by indicating turnings southward to Weymouth, northward to Cerne Abbas (ie, Sherborne), but with no mention of any other road connexion, not even to Blandford. Ogilby said that the route 'in most places, though something hilly, affords an indifferent good way' which was perhaps not dissimilar to Miss Fiennes' contemporary description of 'stony and very narrow'. The western end of Ogilby's route from Exeter was a coastal one, running south of the main London road through Honiton and Axminster and, corresponding with the A35, by Clyst St Mary, Newton Poppleford and Colyford. At the latter (Stukeley's ancient London road), Ogilby degraded the Fosseway connexion to Axminster with a direction 'to several farms' and evidently at that time the old throughway was out of service. The road entered Dorset at Lyme Regis (Illus. 13) and therefore seemed substantially the same as the present A35 in its passing between Bridport and Dorchester. The most recent re-study of the Gough map of 1360 has noted traces of a coastal road between Lyme and Bridport. Thus there seems confirmation of this recognized throughway, which would possibly have continued eastwards, as Leland travelled 200 years later, by Weymouth to Wareham.

There is no evidence as to the particular road taken by

Miss Fiennes, whose description did not suggest the downs, though she mentioned no villages. It is worth taking note of her reference to the 'very narrow road'. She expanded on the theme as she travelled west. Around Lyme

The ways are also difficult by reason of the very steep hills up and down ... and full of large smooth pebbles that make the strange horses slip and uneasy to go: ... in the opener ways they use a sort of waine or carriage made narrower than our southern waggon but longer and so load them high ... into Devonshire the ways very narrow so as in some places a coach and waggons cannot pass; they are forced to carry their corn and carriages on horses' backs with frames of wood like panniers on either side the horse, so load it high and tie it with cords ... the farther westward the ways grow narrower and narrower on to the Land's End.

Of the other, earlier pre-turnpike travellers Defoe took the coast road to Weymouth, Abbotsbury and Bridport. His visit to Dorchester was made from Weymouth. He continued to Lyme. It can be added that of the three Ogilby routes which reached the Dorchester neighbourhood, one of them was that which has been pursued from London, passing Dorchester as a stopping-place on the way to Weymouth; one was this byroad from Exeter to Dorchester: the third was a route from Bristol to Weymouth which gave the county town a final insult by bypassing it a few miles away. The evidence so far is neither in favour of Dorchester as a road centre nor of the A35 route as the main western throughway. And that, with the coastal road, accounts for two of the five alternatives that have been mentioned.

Now both these routes seem to be pre-Roman ridgeways, a point confirmed by the absence of villages on them. The ways on either side of the A35 must be sought for villages, which in this hilly part of the world must represent Saxon and later valley settlements. One very simple route, starting from Dorchester, proceeds along the A35 till it bends left

towards Winterborne Abbas. Here it keeps south to the
Bride valley from Little Bredy to Burton Bradstock and so
to West Bay or Bridport. The other village route toils up
Askerswell Down on the A35, when it turns right to a series
of charming hamlets, Loders and Bradpole and Dottery and
Marshwood, that lead through to Axminster without going
near Bridport at all. Either of these two routes would have
been open to travellers and pack-horse traders from medieval
times; bad, hilly, sometimes marshy routes, but feasible.

Finally there was the most northerly, the Roman road
over Eggardon, which never fails to excite curiosity as to
its exact course. It is first of all important to inquire its
purpose, for if, as seems certain, the present A35 ridgeway
over Askerswell Down was already there in embryo, why
did not the Romans choose this route, instead of picking
on a far more awkward one over Eggardon? (It must still
be hoped that future excavations at Eggardon will disclose
a form of life there in keeping with its truly magnificent
setting. To date they have been woefully insignificant, in no
manner akin to the city-state at Maiden Castle a few miles
away.) Seekers for hard-core Roman roads are satisfied
that the way to Eggardon from Dorchester, though no
doubt Celtic in origin, was thoroughly Romanized, but it
disappears just south of the old fortress when on a line to
the Spyway and Askerswell, and is only thought to re-
emerge near Bridport, where the A35 is said to represent its
course. If that is so, it all seems to have been rather a fuss
about nothing, and somehow not quite in keeping with the
engineering common-sense which seems to epitomize Roman
thinking.

In a consideration of the Roman attitude it must be clear
that their strategy at this point would be dominated by the
recognition that they had come to the end of the flat country
in their westward progress, and that pacification required a
different form of soldiering – more akin to that of the
British in the 1800s on India's North-West Frontier. In
order to keep the main A35 open and protected, it was
necessary to picket the Eggardon heights and the farther

heights westward, such as Lambert's Castle near Lyme and Axminster, where the Roman network was joined by the Fossway from Cirencester through Ilchester. Eggardon would thus become a lookout point within easy reach and signal of the garrison at Dorchester. There would be a road through the hills, made firm and secure from surprise. It would run from Eggardon past the fort and so to the high ground above Nettlecombe, which surely is the obvious place for any road to aim at; it would continue to Mangerton and then, probably by tracks that now are lost, but were more numerous on Taylor's old map, towards Dottery and the route leading to Marshwood, which stands directly under Lambert's Castle, and so on to Axminster. The road would in fact have extended from Lambert's Hill, between Dorchester and Eggardon, and Lambert's Castle near Axminster. (Who was Lambert?)

If this route, so exactly outlined, is guesswork, it does not lack support. And let it be added that it is hard nowadays to get the feel of these downs, when ploughing and made-up roads have altered the whole essence and soul of them. But fresh documentary evidence is certainly available.

For example, there is evidence on the likelihood of Roman thoroughfares from the siting of Norman castles, hunting-lodges and monastic buildings. There was a royal manor at Powerstock, visited in the early 1200s by King John, who reached it through Maiden Newton and Dorchester on separate occasions. There were monastic establishments at Bridport, Loders near Powerstock, Chilcombe south of Askerswell (all three on or close to the A35 ridgeway); and at Frampton and Muckleford on the Roman Dorchester–Ilchester road, along the Frome. Edward I used to visit Frampton around 1300. The conclusion from these facts must be that this part of the world was by no means neglected in the Norman settlements; that a quite extensive road network existed, and that the A35 ridgeway was in use.

There is the evidence provided by a closer examination of Ogilby and his road from Exeter to Dorchester. His map

marked the Eggardon road – there is no mistake about it –
'To Axminster'. To make doubly sure, his notes of particular turnings where the traveller on the Exeter road
could easily go wrong specified this road 'To Axminster'.
And this is indeed of value, because the only practical
course to Axminster over Eggardon Hill is the one that
has just been outlined, through Marshwood. It is the sort of
route that might well have been followed by horse-traders
till trains and motor-cars killed that sort of trade. Axminster was shown by Ogilby on another of his routes, as a
town on this great London–Land's End road. It is again
sound evidence that the only eastern side road he gave
there was 'To Dorchester'.

There is another oddity of evidence, from Taylor's map
of the mid-1700s. He marked the way from Dorchester to
Eggardon 'Roman Road', and showed how, as happens today, it forked towards the top of the rise with one branch
running left towards the Spyway and the other right, this
latter branching either past the fort to Powerstock or taking
a wider sweep which in his day led to Beaminster. Now
there is a general belief today that the Roman section was
the left fork towards Spyway, whatever may have happened
to it thereafter. Why, then, did Taylor mark the lettering
of his 'Roman Road' so that it deliberately swung round
with the right branch, the one that led to Powerstock or
Nettlecombe?

And what, finally, did Dr Stukeley, who is so often badly
misquoted, really say in 1723?

A little north of Bridport, I found the great Icening-
street of the Romans going to Dorchester, which I accompanied with no small pleasure. I imagine it goes a
little farther up the country than I had travelled, and
hereabouts may properly be said to begin, probably
meeting the Foss at Moridunum (Seaton, Illus. 12).
In this place it is called the Ridgeway, both as it
rises in an artificial ridge, and as it takes a high ridge all
the way between here and Dorchester, having many val-

leys on both sides. The composition of the road is wholly of flints gathered off the lands, or taken from near the surface: these were laid in a fine bank, and so covered with turf. As I rode along I found it frequently makes great curves to avoid passing over valleys, and industriously keeps on the highest ground, and commands the prospect of the country everywhere: it goes to Eggardon Hill, as they tell me, north of Bridport; and here I suppose is a camp ... they say hereabouts it was cast up in a night's time by the devil, referring to a super-natural agent the effect of Roman wisdom and industry. It enters the city of Dorchester by the north of Winterburn at West-gate. In divers places they have mended it where wore out, by a small slip of chalk and flints, with a shamefull and degenerate carelessness; so that we may well pronounce the Romans worked with shovels, the moderns with teaspoons: besides it is mostly inclosed and obstructed with perpetual gates across it, to the great hindrance of travellers, to whom public ways ought to be laid open and free; and the authors of such nuisances may well be declared sacrilegious. An endless fund of Celtic as well as Roman inquiries hereabouts, and no where less regarded.

More graphic clues than those are unlikely to appear, and why they should have remained hidden is hard to say. The description of the enclosed downland with its gates across the old ways exactly describes the Dorset downs in these parts up to the ploughing campaigns of the 1940s: in a limited area it has been met within the past ten years. So Stukeley's Roman ridgeway was not the main A35, not even in Bridport. It ran north of Bridport and avoided the valleys, which means its course lay either north or south of the stream at Bradpole.

Taylor's map of 1765 is interesting on the Ridgeway name. He showed only one Ridgeway, the well-known one cutting across the Dorchester–Weymouth road south of Maiden Castle, across Whaddon Down and on the cross-tracks at

Blackdown Hill. So far there is no difference from the route given in the modern *Ancient Trackways of Wessex*. But at Blackdown the modern book bends the main coastal Ridgeway back to its end at Abbotsbury, while two other minor tracks complete the 'cross'. Taylor's map made a different picture, of a normal crossways, with the Abbotsbury road running eastwards to Martinstown and the Whaddon Down road continuing towards Eggardon, crossing the A35 immediately north of Long Bredy. The track continued above Stancombe to the Eggardon road at the exact point where it forks left and right of the Eggardon fort, and quite clearly it was taking the right fork which was the one he deliberately marked 'Roman Road'. And although this track continued northwards to Beaminster, he had a distinct branch which led westwards, apparently on the higher ground immediately north of the stream, by Powerstock and West Milton to Mangerton. There were only forty years between Stukeley and Taylor, and it is at least possible that this is the route they both noted.

It could be argued from this that the original approach to the Celtic Eggardon fort came along from Blackdown, with the road from Dorchester a later addition. If only the Celts had acted in unison, the enormous strength of these positions – Abbotsbury on the coast, Maiden Castle with Poundbury on the Frome crossing, Chilcombe and Eggardon – all covering the A35 approach from the west, would barely have yielded even to the master military machine that Rome alone could furnish. But once Maiden fell, with the Blackdown crossroads behind it, the way was open.

There is at any rate a case here for seeing the accepted Ridgeway route of the 1700s as something that started east of the Dorchester–Weymouth road, continued over Blackdown to Eggardon and then (as described by Stukeley) maintained its course north of the A35 to a point north of Bridport.

Whatever the origin of this road, it was certainly well recognized by its junction with Dorchester from Eggardon, and in Ogilby's time it ran to Axminster. Some fifty years later it was still in active use, as Stukeley showed in his complaints about the sheep gates. To Stukeley it was called the Ridgeway near Bridport, and thus it might conceivably have joined Taylor's Ridgeway around Eggardon. Both these eighteenth-century antiquarians thought that their ridgeways had a Roman background, though there is no present proof of this.

John Hutchins, the Dorset historian, with a first edition in 1774 and amendments well into the 1800s, and others such as John Britton and E. W. Brayley (*Beauties of England and Wales*, 1803), stated that four miles west of Dorchester, where the Roman section broke away from the turnpike to ascend Eggardon Hill, it was known as the Ridgeway and formed part of Icknield Street. At the hill-top, said Hutchins, it was 'flint covered with turf, flat stones placed on the borders, with a ditch on each side'. Some held that the route lay towards Askerswell, others to Powerstock.

Although the naming of Powerstock has been wrongly attributed to Stukeley, such a route would tally – as would the method of construction – with his observations from Bridport already quoted. It is worth noting also that C. Warne in his *Ancient Dorset*, 1872, recorded a Coldharbour site between Eggardon and Powerstock.

Whichever route the Roman, and Ogilby's later Axminster, roads took, the section between Dorchester and the top of Eggardon Hill continued in active use, though by the early 1800s it had become the 'old road' to Bridport via Vinney Cross. Till 1939 (when it collapsed after a storm) a very old signpost faced the top of the metalled Roman way pointing on one side to 'Askerswell & Bridport' and on the other to 'Wynford Eagle & Maiden Newton'. The downland tracks at that time were all but desolate. Nowadays their successors are well-maintained invitations to tourists.

The A35 on Taylor's map was marked 'turnpike', which is supposed to have been built a few years before his map. It did not, nevertheless, indicate the tollgate at Long Bredy.

At any rate its point of departure from the Eggardon road at Lambert's Hill, which to Taylor was the fourth milestone from Dorchester, was less acute than it is today. Apart from its wiggle to accommodate the village of Winterborne Abbas, it showed the famous roadside Bronze Age Nine Stones nearby as on an exact line with the long, straight stretch leading from Dorchester, just as they are on the modern map, and, even more remarkable, on Ogilby's route of 1675. All this does support the opinion that, whatever rival routes there may have been, the A35 has for thousands of years represented the main southern throughway to the west.

Perhaps this account should finish as it began, with the joke pulled on Master Leland and his Bridport dagger, over 400 years ago. Anything can happen in a country where a man can mistake a length of rope for a blade of iron.

CHAPTER EIGHT

The New Forest and
Poole Heath

COASTAL ROUTES

COMMUNICATIONS between Hampshire and Dorset
remained scanty until the upsurge of Bournemouth about
1840. West Hampshire (the New Forest) developed its own
forms of business, while east Dorset (Poole Harbour) did
the same. Ogilby's 1675 survey linked the two with a comparatively minor London–Poole road through Winchester,
Romsey and Ringwood, with its coastal extension between
Poole and Lymington.

The odd thing is that to Ogilby the link between Lymington and Southampton seemed of no consequence. The
latter appeared as a terminal port in three of his national
roads, but not once did he show a direction from it either
to Lymington or Lyndhurst; only to Redbridge or Ringwood. From Lymington he showed one pointer to 'Hampton'; all the other side roads were either to Ringwood or
just 'the forrest'. Maps of the early 1700s confirm his attitude. The main tendency from the coast was northwards
through Burley and Minstead – salt and other industrial
ways, no doubt – and the Lymington–Lyndhurst–Rum-
bridge (Eling) turnpike did not appear till 1765. It sounds
incredible, but the made-up direct road from Lyndhurst
to Christchurch was as late as 1841, and must have followed
the residential boom along the coast. Halfway between the
two lies Holmsley, where was the nearest railway station
to Bournemouth till the 1860s. In the 1960s it has been
taken away again. The through line to Bournemouth was
only opened in 1888 and still remains.

The New Forest, taken as an area bounded by Southampton Water and the Solent, has been a lively industrial centre from days beyond recorded history. Salt, pottery, charcoal, iron, wines, wool, boats ... Beaulieu, till it was broken up, had been one of the great centres, and it is reasonable to think that the Roman road from Lepe to Eling formed the link both with Southampton and, via Beaulieu, with Lymington or Boldre. In addition Lymington was far more used to commercial water transport than is the case today, and it would be normal to travel from one port to another by sea rather than land. Quite probably, since the waterside there was doing a steady export trade in smuggled cloth long before it imported smuggled brandy, Lymington rather encouraged this form of isolation.

An early route from the coast inland would have run up the Lymington stream to Boldre and Brockenhurst, with a crossing for Eling and Beaulieu. The major, pre-Roman way led along the high ground from Lymington to Burley and was in active use till the 1800s. It passed the Wilverley enclosure by a landmark known as the Wilverley Oak, that some 200 years ago must have been struck by lightning and received the name – which as a stump it still retains – of the Naked Man.

But the literally vital role played by those early roads from Lymington and Pennington has never had the recognition it deserves. Salt is an essential to life, and though nobody seems to know when the Solent saltings were first made, they were certainly active in Saxon-Norman times. As populations grew, so did the need for salting down ever-increasing quantities of beef, which till quite recent years could not be preserved alive through the winter. The contribution of the remote Solent community in providing salt not only for Britain, but in later days (via Poole) for Canada and America as well, was a very massive one. It continued until the 1840s, and Hampshire and its neighbours hold many traditions of saltways, a number of which must lead back to Lymington.

The medieval road picture would have shown the main way westward through the forest as the Roman one from Cadnam, roughly where the present Ringwood A31 runs up to Stoney Cross. When the Roman crossing of the Test at Nursling was neglected, the old road found more useful outlets eastwards from Cadnam, to Romsey and Redbridge. The Nursling route seems to have been followed till the 1300s and may well have continued later, for though there was a bridge at Redbridge at the start of the 1200s it was in a constant state of bad repair and even in 1406 was still a subject of concern. In medieval days, therefore, though there would have been a road from Southampton across Redbridge to Lyndhurst, it would have been a minor one and would not have continued west of Lyndhurst except as a track to Burley. Indeed, as late as 1604 it seems to have been known as the Saltway, out of respect to the major industry west of Lymington.

South of Lyndhurst ran the two roads to Brockenhurst and Beaulieu. The main Brockenhurst highway continued north to Minstead, the mother parish of Lyndhurst, though on a more direct route than it takes today. This highway from Salisbury, or in its day Clarendon, Canterton and Minstead, was the chief road through Lyndhurst, and used to run from Minstead to Pikeshill, where it forked right and left to give the approaches from Emery Down and near the Crown Hotel. The record of 1604 suggests that the 'road leading from Salisbury to Lyndhurst' was the Emery Down one. The two branches continued towards Brockenhurst as they do today, meeting at Goose Green. The area thus enclosed was no doubt the original village of Lyndhurst, comprising the site of the church, the Queen's House and Verderers' Hall and the Crown Hotel, with the old royal park enclosures just outside it.

Before the start of the sea-bathing craze at the end of the 1700s the only main road through the southern part of the forest was that from Lyndhurst to Lymington and along to Christchurch and Poole, together with the minor though fairly direct way from Lymington by Sway to Burley and beyond. Otherwise there were the tracks between the various keepers' lodges, which became the delightful, curly lanes so beloved of tourists. It should be added that the original lodges were somewhat on the grand scale, in tune with the grandeur of those who were styled keepers. The main coast road prided itself on its good condition, even before the turnpikes were introduced.

As regards Southampton, as late as 1830 the best way of reaching the forest was said to be by ferry (steam, without doubt) to a landing-place near Marchwood. Hythe, which accepts the modern ferry on its long pier, was not then popular because of poorer landing facilities. Those who were so old-fashioned as to take carriage from Southampton to Lyndhurst would find it rather a dead end. They could visit Cadnam by the new high road that passed the racecourse; they could take the new road to Burley – and it can still be seen how the later main extension to Christchurch was built as a fork from this earlier one – or they could enjoy the journey through Brockenhurst and Lymington along the coast.

CADNAM TO RINGWOOD

From this review of the low-level routes towards the Solent coast, there remains the problem of the main high-level throughway of the forest, that heavily animal-guarded A31 from Winchester to Romsey, Cadnam and Ringwood, the old London–Poole road. Its route between London and Winchester via Farnham has been discussed in Chapters 3–4; from Winchester it seems to have been a wiggly, unkempt affair until the turnpike was made in the latter half of the 1700s. Even after that the name of Pitt Hill near Winchester had a real and dangerous significance well into the last century.

At Hursley came the turnpike gate and new proprietors, and the contrast over the next stretch demands notice; that same stretch through Ampfield to Romsey which, not long before, had been the miserable Ratlake Lane. This is what

A. Young had to say of it about 1767, after the turnpike was made.

The road from Salisbury to Romsey, and the first four miles from thence to Winchester, I found so remarkable good, that I made particular inquiries concerning their making and mending it. They first lay a foundation of large stones, which they level with smaller ones; then make a layer of chalk on that gravel, and lastly, another of sifted gravel, exceeding fine; and in some places tending towards a sand. It is many miles as level, as firm, and as free from loose stones as any the finest garden walk I ever beheld; and yet the traffic is very great by wagons. But scarcely the print of a wheel is to be seen on it for miles; and I really believe there was not a loose stone to make a horse stumble ...

The road is, without exception, the finest I ever saw. The trustees of that road highly deserve all the praise that can be given ... To management the goodness of it must be owing; for fine as their materials are, yet I have in other counties met with as fine; but never with any that were so firmly united, and kept so totally free from loose stones, ruts and water; and when I add water, let me observe, that it is not by that vile custom of cutting grips for it to run off ... but by rendering the surface so immovably firm, that carriages make no holes for it to settle in; and having everywhere a gentle fall, it runs immediately off. To conclude the whole, it is everywhere broad enough for three carriages to pass each other; and lying in straight lines, with an even edge of grass the whole way, it has more the appearance of an elegant gravel walk, than of a high-road.

The present Winchester–Cadnam route by Romsey must have superseded the earlier Roman route by Nursling in late Norman times as Romsey grew in importance. This Roman way had left Winchester by the Southampton road and had forked off at Otterbourne, crossing the Test at

Nursling and thus to Cadnam in the New Forest. The Norman road met the Roman one at Cadnam and followed roughly the same course up to the pre-Roman encampment at Castle Malwood, and for a further mile along the straight to Stoney Cross. Beyond this point no trace of a Roman road has been found, though there is a short stretch exactly at right angles on either side of its termination. It has usually been considered that it must have continued to Ringwood or Poole Harbour (Hamworthy), perhaps on the same line as the modern road which made use of the foundations when the turnpike was built some 200 years ago. A short stretch of Roman road has in recent years been located near Poole, facing towards Ringwood, though this is not conclusive.

On the other hand, Taylor's pre-turnpike map of the 1750s gave no suggestion of any single route on the uplands from Stoney Cross to Picket Post. It showed a multitude of tracks of which one might be termed a faint ghost of the present road, one ran north of it by Broomy Lodge, while another, equally prominent, wandered round south by the Lodge at Bolderwood. These tracks seemed more concerned with the north–south passage than the east–west. Stukeley (1723) confirmed Taylor: 'I hastened through the New Forest, where I found it necessary to steer by the compass, as at sea ... The intricacies of the road gave one uneasiness.'

Despite that definite evidence, the route in the previous century had seemed far more clear-cut. It was chosen for the heavy military escort, three troops of the Sussex Horse and one of the Dorset Militia, that conducted the captive Duke of Monmouth in 1685 through the forest to London and execution. This impression of a well-defined road is at first sight supported by Ogilby's contemporary scroll survey of 1675, with its series of connected straight lines that might represent the later turnpike. But closer study suggests that from Stoney Cross his route started south of the A31 line, past Bolderwood Lodge, which was to become the home of that Lord Delaware who erected the first

Rufus stone nearby, and then crossed the A31 to the route north of Linford Brook.

In the 1700s the maze of tracks on Taylor's map came together by the top of the hill at Picket Post, when the road straightened out, either to Ringwood as at present, or by a more direct way through Crowe to the Avon south of Ringwood. Picket, Picquet or Picked Post is a term met elsewhere; in this instance it was probably a sighting-post for all the numerous tracks including the one from Burley. At the other end of the high ground, towards Cadnam, the earthen walls of Malwood Castle may have served a similar purpose; it was the site of a beacon.

Ogilby's route at this point, in contrast with the scant details of the preceding few miles, was so carefully delineated that it should be recorded. He had apparently come along the Linford Brook track north of the A31, and showed turnings southward to Burley and separately to 'Peeked'. By the turnings was a symbol like a Maltese Cross that might signify the foundations of some ecclesiastical building. He then came to 'Bonner a vill' (North Poulner?) where his road turned south for a few hundred yards at an exact right angle and then made another right angle which perhaps brought it on to the A31 course down to Ringwood. Beyond Ringwood he mistook the Moors stream for the Avon, which he thought he crossed at Palmers Bridge on the pre-turnpike road.

Unlike its coastal brother in the New Forest, the Ringwood road never seems to have been a well-cherished one. The town itself (Illus. 3), early in the 1700s, was said to be thriving, with good brick houses, and busy with its leather and wool manufactures. Yet a century later a local magazine was complaining that the streets were no longer lighted as they once were; highway robberies were ever more numerous, ever closer to the town; the footpaths were disgraceful; the mail-coach road was ankle deep after a shower.

The mystery of the origin of this Ringwood road, which is as perplexing as any in Wessex, has possibly come about only because of the comparatively late developments of towns at either end which altered the course of the early road. This has already been seen at the north-eastern end, where the growth of Romsey took the road off its original Roman (and indeed pre-Roman) line through Nursling. The same thing can be seen at the south-western end with the growth of Ringwood, and confusion need not have arisen had not eighteenth-century antiquarians decided that Ringwood was a Roman town which must therefore have attracted a Roman road. Ogilby, rather earlier, knew better and said it was Saxon.

Without the distraction of Ringwood the line of this forest road is easy to trace; it was an east–west link with the ridge road that ran from Lymington through Burley to Picket Post. It can be seen in part today running on by Picket Post from the top of the Burley road down towards Crow Hill and Wattonsford on the Avon. Over the ford it would in very early days have connected with places like Hengistbury Head, St Catherine's Hill and Dudsbury encampment, and, avoiding the marshes, would have crossed the little Moors stream to meet the Stour at Parley (Riddlesford) or Ensbury. This can be seen to be on a line from Stoney Cross through Picket Post before the later fork towards Ringwood, and would continue towards Wareham on Poole Harbour.

The line of this route is in fact paralleled, all the way from Winchester, by a line of Iron Age sites at Winchester–St Catherine's Hill, Cranbury, Toothill, the Walls on the Test, Tatchbury, Malwood, Castle Piece and Castle Hill north of Burley, to Dudsbury on the Stour.

Little by little its long-distance value receded as Ringwood expanded under the Saxons. Looked at afresh, Ringwood is oddly sited in relation to the road from Stoney Cross to Poole; it bends backwards. But to its Saxon founders there were neither Poole nor Hamworthy. Wareham was their goal on Poole Harbour, Wimborne their road centre on the Stour. The road from Stoney Cross takes a straightish course to reach Wimborne and Wareham through Ringwood.

What of the Roman port of Hamworthy, with which only one hard-core road has been traced, that from Badbury and Old Sarum? There has been just the one small indication of a road coming in from the New Forest; it was located, with evidence of building activity, south of the Stour at Corfe Mullen. Such a road could have led down from Picket Post through Crowe to Wattonsford, with a fork over Palmers Ford to Corfe Mullen. It is beyond dispute that the Romans were interested in the New Forest at both ends; the end near their port at Hamworthy on Poole Harbour and the end near their major interests radiating from the Itchen. They encouraged an industrial development of the forest, and the big pottery workings at Sloden and elsewhere were within easy reach of the T-junction at Stoney Cross. On a lesser scale there were potteries on Poole Harbour.

The explanation of the vanished section of the hard Roman road could well be that it never existed. A hard core was provided where traffic warranted it, but the well-drained, sandy, forest land made a satisfactory route except for a culvert or two in the valleys. The limited horse or foot traffic that took place for many centuries thereafter would have required only the minimum of upkeep of this hard-trodden way. But it started to break down when wheeled traffic became general at the end of the 1600s, and the trade of Poole with America and Canada threw ever-increasing strains on it. As a thoroughfare it virtually disintegrated, and had no foundations to show where it had been. When the makers of the turnpike came along they selected a natural high ground course that was probably not dissimilar to that of the original road.

The New Forest cannot be left without a brief reference to its greatest mystery of all, the death of William Rufus in 1100. For the traditions that surround it find striking support in this study of the contemporary road systems. There are really two traditions which affect the road, though it is only the one road.

First there is the tradition of the route (the 'King's Lane') by which the cart of Purkis, the charcoal-burner, conveyed Rufus' corpse to Winchester. It can be seen from this review that the death site, by the Rufus stone at Canterton near Stoney Cross, was in no remote part of the forest; on the contrary, it was within almost a stone's throw of the cross between the Winchester road and the Old Sarum–Clarendon road to Lymington. The way to Winchester was engrained so deeply in common memory that to this very day local people can tell of it, how it ran from Canterton to Cadnam, to Copythorne and Nursling, to Chandlers Ford and Otterbourne. But the reason for the memory has long vanished, since there is no such road today. It was, as has been shown, the Roman road which in early Norman times would still have been the main highway.

Secondly there is the tradition that Sir Walter Tyrrell, who was implicated in the affair – though modern opinion has exonerated him – made good his escape by riding west and crossing the Avon at Tyrrell's Ford, which thus received its name. There is no reason to doubt the antiquity of the tradition, like the first one. Stukeley remarked in 1723, 'they tell us at Wattonsford the memory of Tyrrell is still preserved, as passing over there when he unawares shot William Rufus'. What is significant here – and seems to strengthen the tale – is that the actual residents associated Wattonsford, which stood on the early road as already shown, with Tyrrell, and seemed unaware of Tyrrell's Ford, although it is only a short distance downstream. Tyrrell's Ford does not appear on the big-scale maps of the 1700s, but is marked on one dated 1805.

Now the tradition says that Tyrrell was fleeing to France, and although he may not have been fleeing as a regicide, to France he certainly did go. Why should he need to cross the Avon to take ship to France, with Christchurch and other Solent ports open to him? The tradition says that he would not have dared appear so close to the scene of the murder and therefore was riding to Poole. This cannot have been in the original version, since in 1100 there was no such place as Poole. At that time its Roman predecessor at Hamworthy seems to have been inoperative, but he might well have sailed from Wareham, which was in active use.

The tale becomes clear once it is seen in terms of the main road system which was then in being but would fade away in later centuries. Just as there was no mystery about the route to Winchester from the Rufus stone, so there was no mystery in the other end of the road which crossed the Avon at Wattonsford with a branch to a minor ford which would ultimately be named Tyrrell's. The tradition is simply that of the old lost road. As for its name, Shore, in his Hampshire history of 1892, had a note that the ford was in the manor of Avon Tyrrell, held by that family in the fourteenth century. Shore thought that Sir Walter was 'riding for his life' and thus using ways known to his family. It is less sensational to believe that the ford took its name after its later owners, not the particular man, and that the association with Sir Walter only came about later for the entertainment of tourists.

While the name of Sir Walter Tyrrell is now perpetuated in the modern inn that has replaced the older one near the Rufus stone, a far more probable connexion with the period remains unrecognized in the inn a short distance away at Stoney Cross on the main road, the Compton Arms. The traditionally Saxon family of Compton, who still own property in the forest, were for long established at Minstead, near the Rufus stone. At the other end of the old road, by Wattonsford, they were maybe in their residence at Bisterne on the day Sir Walter was setting out to catch his ship.

MAKING TRACKS TO BOURNEMOUTH

The coastal road from Lymington to Christchurch and Poole is one of considerable interest and antiquity. It was an important route in Charles II's time, and was mentioned by Leland in the early 1500s with the mileage between Christchurch and Poole. It ran from Christchurch over Iford bridge and then, although it could have taken shorter or more conventional courses to reach Poole, it deliberately chose what is now the main road through Bournemouth, by Pokesdown and Boscombe, the Lansdowne, the Square, up the hill along Poole Road to Upper Parkstone. At the Lansdowne it had its fork along the Holdenhurst road, and at the Square it had a branch precisely like the modern Wimborne Road up Richmond Hill, with its forks at the cemetery to Wallisdown and Moordown.

The accepted tale about the founding of Bournemouth is that it was a desolate wasteland and haunt of smugglers on which Mr L. D. G. Trengonwell erected a house in 1810. This is a fiction, and the truth is far stranger. For a start, it will be recollected that Hengistbury Head, near Christchurch, and Poole Harbour were both invasion points for pre-Roman peoples, and what used to be called Poole Heath – now Bournemouth – is a home for their relics. But that was a long time before the written records of Tudor days, and yet the place cannot have been entirely deserted. There are, in fact, faint clues, and, as so often happens, a few of them can be found in Taylor's maps of Dorset and Hampshire of the mid-1700s. For even then there were definite trackways or roads over the heathland between Christchurch and Poole, and these tracks were linked with tumuli or barrows which were marked with their particular names. Some of these barrows are known to have been excavated with positive burial evidence, others may have been just landmarks of later date; but the fact that they were associated with roads and had been given names does prove that the heathland must have been in steady use.

There were tracks running inland from the coast, principally at Boscombe Chine, Bournemouth Chine and Alum Chine. All these, though they connected with the east–west tracks more or less parallel to the coast, seemed concerned to reach the River Stour that runs a few miles inland, by

Wimborne and Canford and Didsbury, to reach the sea at
Christchurch. The Stour carries a typical series of Saxon
villages on either bank; Holdenhurst, West Parley and the
rest. Between the river and the sea the western side of the
heath, even today when it is mostly built over, is called
Wallisdown; till the 1800s there were at least two points on
it called Wallisford, on the tributaries of the small Bourne
stream. These two tributaries ran through quite deep valleys and maybe the Bourne, that tiny child's plaything
which runs through the Bournemouth pleasure gardens,
was a more sizable affair till the area was drained.

Elsewhere in England these 'Walli-' names are accepted
as evidence of Celtic survivals into Saxon times, the word
meaning 'Welch' or (to the Saxons) 'foreigner'. So here is
a reasonable case for thinking that the hinterland of Poole
Heath was populated from pre-Roman through to Saxon
days, and it is thus not difficult to see the reason for these
tracks to the coast as a desire for sea food as a change from
river fish or oysters from Poole Harbour. No doubt a similar pattern continued when the Normans took over and
established the extremely powerful manor of Canford extending to the harbour and the Bournemouth coastline. In
1306 Edward I visited Canford and West Parley, when
surely it would have been natural to explore the track that
led to the Bournemouth beaches and so set a fashion that
has been followed by royal Edward into this century.

The track from Alum Chine in West Bournemouth was
one of the chief ways; it descended to the Bourne valley
near the modern Coy (decoy) pond and rose again (Illus.
18) towards Wallisdown, being obviously sighted on an old
mound called Fernbarrow which has long been excavated
so that it presents the appearance of a small bowl. It ran
– for a short distance it was the county boundary – to the
Stour at Redhill (Riddlesford) and so to West Parley by
the Iron Age settlement of Dudsbury. The last vestiges of
these trackways are being surrendered to the builders at this
very moment, and though in some cases their course may
remain, it is often under a fresh name that gives no clue to

its origin. For example, of the three east–west routes, the coastal one through Bournemouth Square, which has already been described, would normally be thought to be modern. The Saxon village route by the Stour is now Castle Lane, a main motor road. The third, between the two, ran across Wallisdown and can still be met in Talbot Road, Alma Road and Richmond Park Road. It was probably the first of the three which subsequently became a short cut from Canford to Christchurch before the growth of Poole in the 1200s encouraged the coast road.

Taylor's Hampshire map of the 1750s marked it 'A Roman Way from Wareham to Christchurch' and its course can be continued on his slightly later Dorset map. It started below Christchurch not far from the pre-Roman town at Hengistbury Head, then ran south of the bridge at Iford past Quants Corner where it was met by the Alum Chine track. It crossed Wallisdown, keeping on the high ground south of East Howe, and so to 'Babdon' and across Canford Heath. It ran, rather north of the new estate and Fleets Bridge Road, to Upton. Here, crossing the Roman road from Badbury to Hamworthy, which its course seemed to ignore as it did any connexion with Poole, it came out on what is now the A35 at the top of the slope west of Upton House. For a short stretch it still exists here, unmade up, approaching the main road at an acute angle (Illus. 18). Even more remarkable, this short stretch has been known all this century till today as 'the Roman road', while the line of the hard Roman road to Hamworthy, a few hundred yards away, is unrecognized.

The way continued close to the shore of Poole Harbour, avoiding Lytchett Minster; clearly it was the route travelled by Leland about 1540 when he noted a short cut to Poole from Wareham by using a ferry across Lytchett Bay. It can still be met near Wareham railway station, joining the main A35 by the bridge at Sandford from the direction of Keysworth Farm.

In the 1500s there were other recorded facts. The actual name of Bournemouth was mentioned at the time of the

Spanish invasion scares in 1574 as a possible landing-place.
A contemporary defence map of the Solent showed it as
possessing a fortification. But shortly before then other
matters had been developing. The lord of the manor of Canford, who still owned much of the land hereabouts, was a
man of some scientific attainment coupled with business
acumen. The products of alum and copperas were in great
demand for dyeing, and he discovered that supplies were
obtainable on his own lands at Parkstone on Poole Harbour and at Alum Chine, on ground he rented at Brownsea
Island in the harbour and at Boscombe, east of Bournemouth. He set to work at his 'mines' and was soon export-
ing the stuff by shipload to London from Poole. Norden's
manuscript map of Hampshire of about 1590 not only outlined Alum and Boscombe Chines with considerable accu-
racy, but indicated their 'Alum and Copperas Houses'.

A hundred years later, about 1700, Celia Fiennes described the Brownsea workings with exact detail, and these
industrial occupations, including the Parkstone iron mills
and the salterns in the neighbourhood of the modern Bee-
hive Hotel, continued on a dwindling scale till about the
end of the eighteenth century, when the choice of a liveli-
hood must have veered between smuggling and opening a
seaside boarding-house.

The Alum Chine trackway, from the chinehead of today's
Warren–Alumhurst roads, would have been given a new
impetus by this industry, with a commuting of mine-
workers towards Wallisdown where the old fishermen's route
had a link with Kinson and Canford. While it has never become a built-up road to East Howe or Redhill (where till
quite recently there remained a ferry over the Stour), its
parallel westerly track has for a long time been in active
use as Alder Road. Northwards it continues to East Howe,
dropping down to the Stour along what seems so incongru-
ous in the midst of all this modern development, a sunken
lane. Probably it crossed the river at Ensbury and once led
to the ancient encampment at Dudsbury. Towards the coast,
Alder Road takes course along Branksome Chine or the

Canford Cliffs Road that arose from Sandy Lane after the 1914 War; both have well-established connexions with smuggling.

The tale can be brought right into the 1900s as a continued link at any rate as far back as the Norman owners of Canford manor. The very name Canford Cliffs, that wealthy suburb of Poole/Bournemouth, comes from it, and as 'Canford Lawnes' it appeared on a Tudor map, complete with stags. On the county boundary, between Alum Chine and Branksome Chine, the first Lord Wimborne, who had purchased the Canford estate in the late 1800s, built himself a handsome seaside mansion called Branksome Dene. The house, with its fine Italian ceilings, became a vegetarian hotel in the 1920s at about the same time that Canford manor house, near Wimborne, became a boys' public school. But a final feudal note had been struck before then by a private road that stretched from Canford itself across Canford Heath towards Wallisdown, Bournemouth and Branksome Dene, with its private bridge over the main turnpike A348 from Poole to Ringwood and London. The private road emerged through its massive gates near Alder Road with its old barrow landmarks, Astney and Lush, Baldwin's Grave and the rest.

As for Bournemouth itself, it has been shown that the name has been in use at any rate from the reign of Elizabeth I. There seems no case for the Tregonwell claim to have founded it with his house in 1810, even as a resort. Boscombe had its Boscombe Lodge long before that, while maps and other documents show that the Bourne stream was certainly bridged by 1800 and there were dwellings roughly opposite Trinity Church and by the Arcade. The old Tregonwell Arms that stood just below the present Criterion Hotel was in fact the rebuilding of an earlier inn, the Tapps Arms, named after the owners of the land.

Tregonwell's house was built on an existing public way, now Exeter Road, from the Square to the pier; it seems to have been nameless till 1820 when it was let to the Marchioness of Exeter and was called Exeter House, part of it being incorporated in the Exeter Hotel. It could have been named Bourne House because a Bourne House was standing there long before Tregonwell was born in 1758. It was a permanent checkpoint in all the road guides of the period. Its last days were spent as a derelict building associated with smugglers and sportsmen; at the turn of the century there was a decoy pond just above the Square where the Memorial Gardens stand. It might perhaps have been a link with the alum and copperas workings, a central distribution warehouse and overseer's residence.

Much of the historic importance of the Bournemouth or Poole Heath area has tended to become overlooked because it was a no-man's-land with a fluid boundary line on the borders of Dorset and Hampshire. The county line, not much more than 100 years ago, was usually reckoned as the Bourne stream or just westward at Durley Chine; without doubt it was a Dorset sphere of influence from the great manor of Canford. Its industrial interests were fading away by the end of the 1700s but its pioneers as a pleasure resort preceded Tregonwell and were the landowners (the Tapps family), the occupants of Boscombe Lodge, and the unknown host of the Tapps Arms, near the Square, who used his wayside inn on the Poole–Lymington road as a means of encouraging picnic and bathing parties at quite an early stage.

Bournemouth the resort started to be recognized from about 1838 with the new main road to Christchurch. Robert Mudie's *Hampshire*, published in 1840, said, 'At the mouth of the Bourne there are decoys for wild fowl ... to the east is the villa of Boscombe, a dwelling in the wilderness'. In 1846 came H. Moody's *Sketches of Hampshire*, and internal evidence shows that the following extract cannot have been written earlier than 1845: 'The fashionable watering place of Bournemouth ... Within a few years a handsome and spacious hotel, a range of commodious baths and a series of elegant villas have been erected.'

CHAPTER NINE

Portsmouth Harbour

THE WESTERN APPROACHES

THE high downland along the Hampshire coast provides one of the oldest roads in Britain, and no doubt the creeks of Portsmouth Harbour have offered nourishment to very remote peoples. It is suspected, for example, that Roman Porchester had a pre-Roman background, and certainly the way from there to the top of Portsdown Hill must have been trodden from very early times.

In Roman days their coastal roads eastwards from Southampton by Wickham and Havant towards Kent would have served both a defensive and a trading purpose, though the great port at Porchester was not built till towards the end of their occupation, when Saxon incursions were growing ever stronger and bolder. There would have been a link from this coastal road to the harbour fortress, and there was a further link from the Wickham neighbourhood to Winchester by Owslebury and Morestead. Common-sense would suggest one more link from Wickham up the Meon valley towards the Chichester–Silchester road, though it might only have needed a strengthening of existing trackways. The tale of Carausius, who for a time controlled Britain in defiance of Rome, of his murder by Allectus and the subsequent re-invasion by Rome around 296, is all centred between Chichester, Porchester and the Selborne area, and its mystery can only be solved in terms of good communications.

With the withdrawal of Roman troops came the Anglo-Saxon invasion when (though it is still disputed) the separate race of Jutes is said to have occupied the Meon valley

and the coastal area of the Solent on both sides of Southampton Water, as well as the Isle of Wight. The evidence
shows the Jutes as living on friendly terms with the Saxons
until ultimately absorbed by them, but always – and it is
claimed that traces of this can be found even down to the
present day – trying to keep their separate identity. Such an
attitude is borne out by the evidence of road systems, which
suggest a deliberate break between Jute-land and Saxon-
land. It can be noticed in the New Forest and can be seen
in the apparent absence of a major medieval throughway
from Alton to West Meon.

The Jutes must have resented the excellent existing Roman road network which would discourage their desire for
isolation. They might of course have broken up long
stretches, though this is pure conjecture. A curiosity about
the Roman traces can be noticed in the large-scale Ordnance
drawings made about 1800, which show virtually nothing
of the coastal Southampton–Wickham road, but mark the
ridge of the Winchester road almost all the way to a point
west of Waltham.

When did this Roman Southampton–Wickham–Havant
road, a portion of which constitutes today the A333 east
of Wickham between North Boarhunt and Walton Heath,
go out of use? An early clue can be found in the Gough
map of Britain compiled about 1360; one of its few
southern roads ran from Southampton south of Waltham
and north of Portsmouth towards Havant and Chichester.
This certainly suggests that the Roman road or substantial
parts of it were still in being, and that it was an important
thoroughfare which Edward I is recorded as following in
1297. At that time cross-Channel traffic would have been
considerable, and indeed the map-compilers would have regarded England and Normandy as one. But their road continued as far as Canterbury and probably reflected the
extraordinary mystical emphasis that was placed on a pilgrimage to the shrine of Thomas à Becket.

The Roman thoroughfare may have been abandoned,
stretch by stretch, as settlements off its course, such as Botley,

grew in importance. But from Norman times onwards there was never a period when conditions did not demand an easy flow of traffic between Southampton and Portsmouth, and routes through Wickham or Fareham must always have been open. To later travellers the attraction of either route seemed to lie, not in the villages, but in a choice of two private estates. There was the magnificence of Titchfield on the one road and the wooded beauty of Southwick on the other. Stukeley, travelling in 1723 along Portsdown Hill (which he termed the London road) noted 'some of the Roman way upon this ridge, and a large long barrow'. The main Roman road went near Southwick.

THE BISHOPS' ROAD
FROM WINCHESTER TO WALTHAM

From late Saxon times the need for communication between Winchester and Portsmouth Harbour continued to expand until the great Norman castle was built at Porchester, with other developments in Portsmouth itself, towards the end of the 1100s. During that period and maybe till later the Roman Winchester–Wickham road would have carried the traffic. But another factor was being introduced into the area by the growing popularity of Waltham as a residence for the bishops of Winchester. They developed it as an enclosed sporting estate of some 1,000 acres, which, according to an Elizabethan map, extended northwards nearly as far as Upham and must thus by the look of it have included part of the Roman road.

A hint of the connexion between Waltham Palace and this road is shown in an early map prior to the modern Waltham–Twyford road. There was a winding lane from the palace to Trullingham Farm and Old Farm nearby. A short straight lane ran northwards from here along the actual Roman road; it still seems to be the same short stretch as that shown on the present 2½-inch Ordnance map leading to Wintershill Farm.

The Winchester end of the Roman highway appears always to have remained in use through Morestead as far as

Owslebury. It was recorded some fifty years ago that from a point somewhere near today's bypass the sides of the road as far as Owslebury were scored with deep tracks suggesting heavy medieval traffic. They might have been related to the early days of sledge transport, quite possibly connected with the haulage of timber for buildings in Winchester. The scores could have ceased at Owslebury where the trees were cut down.

It is here that emerges one of the most curious paradoxes that can be met in this or any other county. It is concerned with the few short miles between Owslebury and Waltham where the Roman road has been completely abandoned. For some five or six hundred years that small stretch of country knew, not occasionally but day in and day out, the passage of the most famous overlords in England. It saw Richard Coeur de Lion on his last English journey; Henry V leaving for Agincourt; Henry VIII riding with Charles V of Spain. It saw their queens and their courts, their jesters and their attendants; the great prelates of Canterbury and York and Winchester – Wolsey, de Blois, William of Wykeham.

When William, a local man famed for his road-making, died, his body was borne from Waltham to Winchester, and pennies were distributed wherever the cortège stopped. Surely all that is enough to form a tradition of the road? Yet there seems no shred of a tradition. Perhaps a tradition required a violent death like that of the wretched Rufus in the New Forest.

The need for this medieval bishops' road would have disappeared at about the end of the 1600s, when the palace at Waltham had already been destroyed by Cromwell and the park was broken up and leased out in farm units. By the mid-1700s the Gosport turnpike was made, branching off at Morestead and around Stephens Castle Down. Later came the modern Portsmouth road through Twyford. It will be noted that both these roads avoid the direct course to Waltham, and it could be that the old tracks leading round by Stephens Castle Down, which became the turnpike, represented the public right of way round the bishops' park, while the direct route through the park was marked 'strictly private'. The boundary of the park, known as the 'lug', was no mean thing; 6 ft high, 16½ ft broad, with trees planted on the top. There seem no traces of it today, though one has been located near Fishers Pond that may have been connected with Marwell Hall.

Up to the early 1700s the bishops' road seems to have been still in use. Ogilby's 1675 scroll route of the London–Southampton road shows at Morestead crossroads a direction to Owslebury and Waltham; while about 1720 there are two small-scale maps both showing a minor road from Winchester to Morestead, then just east of Owslebury, on to Waltham, and so to Wickham, Fareham and Cosham to join the main London–Portsmouth road.

This must have been the route followed in 1685 by James II, who was probably the last king to use it, on his visit to Winchester shortly after he had come to the throne. John Evelyn recorded that they went to Portsmouth with the king 'riding on horseback a good part of the way'. When Evelyn departed the king 'was pulling on his bootes in ye Towne-Hall, and tooke horse for Winchester'. These equestrian references provide a clue that in those days there was not enough heavy traffic to justify even the suggestion of a main road between Winchester and at any rate Bishops Waltham. But for some reason the Roman road had been neglected, and there must have been a more or less direct route for all these dignataries to follow. Its most likely course is that now given.

The present way from Winchester which follows the Roman road passes through Morestead and then takes the right fork to Owslebury. At the end of the straight it bears left steeply uphill (the Roman line going right) and at the top is a most unexpected memorial. The signpost that confronts the traveller looks as if it should have come out of a museum, though it may be hoped that it is many a long year before it reaches one. It is made of cast iron with the lettering all in one block, and the 'Arlesford' road (with the old spelling) to which it points is one through Tichborne that seems to have gone out of practical use in the first half of the 1800s.

From this signpost the route turns left away from Owslebury for a matter of a few yards, and then right again towards Baybridge and Upham. It is impossible not to be impressed by the signs of antiquity along this lane, especially after it passes the few houses and then drops downhill along that remarkable straight course which might well have been in use long before the Romans built their parallel road to the right. Towards its foot will be seen the valley road coming in on the left from Cheesefoot Head. This is the route that Cobbett was following on one of his rides in 1823, when he gave the lie to current local opinion which maintains that the pronunciation of 'Owslebury' has always been 'Osslebury'. Cobbett, who left an impression that he did not know the place and was quoting the dialect of a neighbouring farmer, twice spelt it 'Ouselberry'. The Waltham route took the right-hand valley road which continues up the next hill to Upham. Here (ignoring the modern signposts) it was aiming at the far southern end of the village which can most surely be found by keeping to the left-hand fork where it was entered. Beyond the Brushmakers Arms it arrives at a road T-head and some of the ground in front towards Bishops Waltham must be that which was part of the bishops' park; a sort of no-man's-land. Old maps show two ways of crossing it, partly navigable today. One of them drops down the hill from the Upham T-head past Ashton, where there was once a chapel, and Vernon Hill to the palace; the other goes right by Stakes Farm and Cross Lane Farm to the same point.

A great deal of space has been devoted to this short stretch of road, but it is justified. The remaining sections of these roads to Portsmouth Harbour are clear enough and well documented. This royal or episcopal route between Owslebury and Waltham Palace should be equally well known, yet there seems no detailed reference to it anywhere.

Perhaps there are archives within or without the walls of Winchester that can settle the issue.

It seems rather sad if there is no record of great William of Wykeham's last journey, where his funeral pence were scattered to those who came to mourn him. A prophet is not without honour, save in his own time and in his own country.

THE LONDON – PORTSMOUTH ROAD

Most road numbers in Hampshire begin with the figure 3, conforming to the system that all roads shall be so prefixed which start between the trunks A3 (Portsmouth road) and A4 (Bath road). Thus the Portsmouth road is pre-eminent in county classification, a dignity that it has enjoyed for 300 years, probably 400. By contrast with others less honoured, it could be regarded as a bit of a mushroom.

The stretch between London and Guildford was borrowed from the much older road from London to Winchester and Southampton, which seems to have taken to the Bagshot route at about the time that Portmouth's supremacy as a naval base was being established. It is not so easy nowadays to recognize that till very recently Surrey was a close member of the Wessex tradition, with its religious life administered from the see of Winchester and the bishops of Winchester having two great houses in Farnham and Southwark. Nobody would doubt the connexion who has read of the close interest taken by the medieval bishops of Winchester in the affairs of Surrey, as for example this new endowment of the vicarage at Kingston-on-Thames in 1376–7 – 'it shall be lawful for the vicar to keep a school for boys, to teach reading, writing, plain song and Latin . . .'

Ogilby's 1675 description of the route from London is worth considering

From the Standard in Cornhill, down Gracechurch Street, Fish Street Hill, over London Bridge and through

Southwark, you come to Newington well frequented by the neighbouring citizens ... you pass by Clapham whence over Battersea Heath into Wandlesworth vulgo Wansworth ... to Putney Heath leaving the bowling green on the right you come to New Park enclosed with a stone wall (Richmond Park); whence passing over the hill, not rarely infested by robbers, into Kingston super Thames ...

And so by Esher to Cobham ('well furnished with inns') and between two ponds and some iron mills on the right (Wisley pond and near the gardens of the Royal Horticultural Society), to Ripley and Guildford on the River Wey, 'made navigable from this place by the help of sluices'. It is entertaining to note the directories of the route 100 or 150 years later, when Georgian England had reached its peak. The new exclusive villas were swamping Wandsworth, Battersea and Putney, and hardly a house but had its titled occupant.

Beyond Guildford the central stretch of the Portsmouth road, over Hindhead, was one that travellers always dreaded and tried to avoid by a detour through Haslemere between Godalming and Liphook. The final stretch, between Petersfield and Cosham, over Butser, seems a later alternative for the very old road by Buriton to Havant which will be discussed shortly. To encourage the direct route, permission for a turnpike between Portsmouth and Sheet (Petersfield) was given at the early date of 1710, long before the general Wessex run of turnpikes. But people still continued to use the Havant way, and in due course the railway paid it the compliment of following it closely. The various roads can be seen with the help of Samuel Pepys, the conscientious naval secretary who enjoyed his Portsmouth, which tactfully made him a Freeman.

In 1661 he went from London by Leatherhead to Godalming for the night, then to Petersfield. This seemed a good way to avoid Hindhead. Fifty-odd years later Defoe was recommending the same thing. 'From Guildford there lies a cross-road to London,' he wrote, 'not frequented by coaches or carriages, or the ordinary passengers to London; tho 'tis by some reckoned the nearest way, and is without question much the pleasanter road.' It ran to Leatherhead over Banstead Downs or, slightly longer but an even better road, through Epsom.

In 1662 Pepys went from London to Guildford for the night, then to Petersfield 'and thence got a countryman to guide us by Havant, to avoid going through the Forest; but he carried us much out of the way'. Little remains of the Forest of Bere, though once it was a grim part of the thickly wooded wealden area that made the Sussex roads so notorious. It might have been equally thick along the old road from Buriton, but perhaps not so deep or so bleak.

Buriton was the mother parish of Petersfield, and it is easy to see why. In the events of early history the creeks along the Langstone and Portsmouth harbours would have been populated well before the promontory of Portsmouth itself. Along the top of the downs ran the pre-Roman east–west main road, and it is not being fanciful to see an early route from the Havant or Hayling Island shore going northwards over the hill, past the future sites of Buriton and Petersfield, and thus towards Alton and beyond. Certainly the road would have been developed in Saxon times, and made even more useful by the Roman coastal road westwards from Chichester through Havant. The siting of Buriton, snug at the foot of the hill, would be a natural one; Petersfield would only have developed later as a road centre in the wide valley, when communications and population were expanding and a market became necessary. The stone village of Buriton is worth a visit in its own right.

The course of the old road is quite clear. From the centre of Petersfield the turning is roughly a mile along the A3 towards the coast. There is a signpost on the left, and nowadays a motorist will turn into the lane without being aware of what is coming. One moment he is on the broad modern suburban highway and the next he is back in ancient Britain. Mr Pepys' countryman could not possibly have gone wrong at the Buriton end, for the way is so deeply sunken that there is no alternative.

It went up the hill (Illus. 17), under the railway bridge, and then kept east of Chalton Down by Finchdean to (Norman) Rowlands Castle. Old maps show such a maze of tracks around this forest area that the countryman could easily have lost himself. Certainly by the 1700s the then rare privilege of a signpost had been given to the cross-roads just south of Rowlands Castle, near the Robin Hood Inn. For it continued as a popular route in spite of turnpike improvements to the main Butser road. The great engineer Telford was in Portsmouth towards the end of the 1700s, but as late as the 1820s the guide books were still selling Butser hard, with 'the extensive vale of the forest of Bere, not, as it anciently appeared, impervious and gloomy, but shining in all the radiance of civilized cultivation'.

TO PORTSMOUTH FROM THE MIDLANDS

In Pepys' time the important cross road from Oxford to Petersfield and thence to Portsmouth and Chichester was well established. It ran through Newbury, Basingstoke and Alton (see Chapter 5, 'Roads from Oxford'); thence to Chawton and East Tisted. From Alton the old road continued along what is now the A32 as far as Hedge Corner about a mile beyond East Tisted, where it forked left to Petersfield or right to Ropley and Alresford. It had no defined status south of that point except a couple of tracks leading anywhere but West Meon. A shorter and seemingly more popular way cut off diagonally near East Tisted, leaving Colemore on its right. It met the Hedge Corner–Petersfield road which thereabouts was called 'the Barnett' (Illus. 16), a word that means land cleared by burning. Barnet Side Farm still exists. At the top of Stoner Hill it took the present right fork past Weekgreen Cottage and then swung eastwards again towards Stoner House. The whole route was straightened out as a turnpike in the last century with its famous zigzag descent down Stoner Hill.

An important alternative, instead of going to Petersfield itself, led round Steep to Sheet, coming out by the Portsmouth road bridge over the Rother which even in the 1600s was made of stone. This was a recognized upland route between Winchester, Alresford and the Chichester direction. Although the Petersfield–Winchester valley road (roughly the A272) was in existence, it seems to have had a terrible reputation. The way through Steep was probably earlier and better going.

THE NEW PORTSMOUTH ROAD
THROUGH FARNHAM

It might be thought that the roads to the harbour already discussed would have been enough. Yet as late as 1826 another route was offered to the traveller, and it must have been a costly venture since many miles of it cut straight across untapped ground, wooded at that. The southern end of it is that which is known today as the A325 from Farnham to Liss and Petersfield.

The curious thing about this road, the new Portsmouth road as it was bravely termed, was that it left London by the main Southampton route via Bagshot to Farnham, which seems a long way round. The coaching guides of the period were definite that the mileage from London to Portsmouth by either road was exactly the same, though the more inquisitive would find that the measurements were taken from two different points and that there was a cunning deception at Petersfield about old and new milestones. But if the net result was to cut out the horrors of Hindhead, who was to grumble?

The paradox of it all is that, as has been shown in Chapter 4, 'Bagshot to Farnham', the main Portsmouth road made use of the old Southampton route from London to Guildford. The new Portsmouth road followed the Southampton route through Bagshot at exactly the same moment that travellers to Southampton (Jane Austen was one of them) were deciding it was really much nicer to go round by Guildford. And this is the reason why the road at Bagshot by the Jolly Farmer Inn is called the Portsmouth road instead of the Southampton road.

There must have been high hopes for this new road, because the section from Farnham was cut through Alice Holt and Wolmer forests, wild lands avoided by earlier travellers. It was by Woolmer pond, where, as is now known, the Roman road from Silchester to Chichester crossed the modern thoroughfare, that Gilbert White recorded the finding in 1740 of a considerable number of Roman coins. They continued to turn up until in 1873 the first Lord Selborne at nearby Blackmoor found 30,000 of them – the largest collection ever located in Britain.

Stukeley had noticed this Roman road at Chichester in 1723, but thought it went to Winchester. Certainly it was the route (Chichester, Wolmer, Selborne, Old Basing) followed by Edward I in 1285 and it probably stayed in partial use till the break-up of Selborne Priory in 1486. Commonsense insists that there should have been a link between this road and the Porchester locality, and a further note on it is given at the end of this chapter.

THE GOSPORT ROADS

A brief reference has already been made to the Winchester–Gosport road through Bishops Waltham and Wickham. The major London–Gosport road was planned in 1780 to make use of part of that system. It followed the Southampton road as far as Alton and then branched down through Chawton and East Tisted, corresponding here with the route that was taken by the much earlier Oxford–Petersfield–Portsmouth road. But instead of turning off at Hedge Corner to Petersfield it went on to West Meon and originally reached Gosport via Bishops Waltham. The section of the A32 through Droxford seems to have been a later improvement. The great McAdam himself is said to have been concerned with this Gosport road, at any rate at the Alton end.

In fact it all seems to have been a bit of a hotch-potch

affair. In the French wars Gosport had been growing apace, and no doubt while they lasted the turnpike revenues justified the venture. But after that its future was doubtful, like that of the later Meon Valley railway which barely lasted sixty years. Certainly the essential link between Corhampton and Bishops Waltham was made under a different schedule, one of the strangest of all the turnpikes. About the year 1800 Southampton was feeling ambitious and decided to promote a direct London–Southampton road which would cut out Winchester, take the Waltham highway, and branch from there over Beacon Hill on Preshaw Down and thence to Filmore Hill to join the Gosport road near Privett, south of East Tisted.

A condition of the permit was that a branch should be run from Waltham to Corhampton, a much more southerly point on the Gosport road. The branch was therefore built first and is the B3035 route in use today. The great venture over Beacon Hill never came off, and like many others the turnpike trust was finally wound up as bankrupt. But the course it proposed to follow was hopefully described in the period guide books as though it had already become a first-class road, and though this never happened the original route over Wheeley Down is still in existence.

Its course ran from Alton down the A32, and going south after East Tisted passed the present Pig and Whistle Inn. Then follows a crossroads (West Tisted and Privett), and immediately after that a lane forks off to the left. That was how the coach road used to go till well into last century. A short distance along it there is a right turn, where till quite recently stood not only the present small inn but a larger one as well. This is Filmore Hill, and the A32 main road is now in front. Across it is the early road which has just been described, and it can be seen that the big A32 going through the middle down to the West Meon Hut is an obvious newcomer. The old road (now signposted Woodlands) continued past the old Three Horseshoes Inn, now a private house, and down the hill, crossing the A272 and ascending to Wheeley Down and Beacon Hill past the

lovely copper beeches of Brockwood House. A branch
could certainly have run towards Porchester, as even today
its main direction is clearly to Bishops Waltham at one end
but equally clearly is not to East Tisted and Alton at the
other. At Filmore Hill its course was towards Farnham and
it went by Basing Park and Selborne Priory, crossing the
Roman Chichester–Silchester road. The Winchester bishops,
travelling from Waltham Palace, must have known it well.

Bibliography

TRAVELLERS THROUGH WESSEX

Stukeley, William. *Itinerarium Curiosum*. 2nd edition, 1776.

Young, A. *A Six Weeks' Tour through the Southern Counties of England and Wales*. 3rd edition, 1772.

Leland's Itinerary in England and Wales. c 1535–43. Edited by L. T. Smith. Centaur Press, 1964.

Samuel Pepys' Diary. London, 1871.

Hudson, W. H. *A Shepherd's Life*. 12th edition. Methuen, 1932.

Hudson, W. H. *Afoot in England*. Dent, 1929.

The Journeys of Celia Fiennes. Cresset Press, 1947.

Defoe, Daniel. *A Tour through the Whole Island of Great Britain*. Dent, 1962.

Anon. *A Tour through the South of England* 1791. Edwards, London.

Cobbett, W. *Rural Rides*. Dent, 1948.

John Evelyn's Diary. c 1640–1700. 2nd edition, 1819.

ROAD TRAVEL AND CONSTRUCTION

Young, A. *A Six Weeks' Tour* (see above).

Gregory, J. W. *The Story of the Road*. Maclehose, 1931.

Oliver, Jane. *Ancient Roads of England*. Cassell, 1936.

Jervoise, E. *Ancient Bridges of Southern England*. Architectural Press, 1930.

Scott-Giles, C. W. *The Road Goes On*. Epworth Press, 1948.

Bayne-Powell, R. *Travellers in Eighteenth-Century England*. Murray, 1951.

Belloc, Hilaire. *The Road*. British Reinforced Concrete Engineering Co Ltd, 1923.

HISTORY

History of the King's Works. HM Stationery Office, 1963.

Shore, T. W. *History of Hampshire*. Elliott Stock, 1892.

Milner, Rev A. B. *History of Micheldever*. Herbert Clarke, Paris, 1924.

Hoskins, W. G. *Local History in England*. Longmans, 1959.

Smith, H. P. *History of Poole*. Looker, 1948.

Beresford, M. *New Towns of the Middle Ages*. Lutterworth Press, 1967.

Grundy, G. B. 'Saxon Land Charters', *Archaeological Journal*, Vol 84.

Cochrane, C. 'A Roman Road in Hampshire', *Courier Magazine*, August 1964.

Wykeham's Register. Edited Kirby. Hampshire Record Society, 1899.

Copley, G. J. *The Conquest of Wessex in the Sixth Century*. Phoenix House, 1954.

Boon, G. C. *Roman Silchester*. Max Parrish, 1957.

Stooks, Rev C. D. *A History of Crondall and Yateley*. Warren, Winchester, 1905.

Seymour and Trower. *Records of Winchfield*. Jacob and Johnson, 1891.

Baring, F. H. 'William the Conqueror's March through Hampshire in 1066', *Hampshire Field Club and Archaeological Society Proceedings*, Vol 7, Part 2. 1915.

Mudie, Robert. *Hampshire*. 1840.

Duthy, John. *Sketches of Hampshire*. 1839

Caesar's War Commentaries. Edited John Warrington. Dent, 1955.

Curtis, William. *The Town of Alton*. Warren, Winchester, 1896.

Harper, C. G. *Historic Inns of Old England*. Burrow, 1927.

Heath, F. R. and Long, E. T. *Dorset* (The Little Guides). 10th edition. Methuen, 1949.

Cunnington, M. E. *Archaeology of Wiltshire*. Devizes, 1934.

Chase of Cranborne. London, 1841.

Benfield, E. *The Town of Maiden Castle*. Hale, 1947.

Tristam, W. O. *Coaching Days and Coaching Ways*. Macmillan, 1901.

Anglo-Saxon Chronicle. Edited G. N. Garmonsway. Dent, 1965.

The Venerable Bede. *Ecclesiastical History of the English Nation.* Dent, 1963.

Moody, H. *Sketches of Hampshire.* Jacob & Johnson, 1846.

Gray Hill, N. 'Excavations on Stockbridge Down', *Hampshire Field Club and Archaeological Society Proceedings,* Vol 13 Part 3. 1939.

The Crypt, An Antiquarian Journal. Ringwood, 1827.

Williams-Freeman, J. P. *Field Archaeology (Hampshire).* Macmillan, 1915.

Burke, Thomas. *The English Inn.* Longmans, 1931.

Itineraries of medieval kings, especially Henry I, John, Henry III and Edward I.

It is impossible to list the hundreds of local and county histories that have been read, always with pleasure, often with benefit, in preparing this book. If the works quoted above show a preponderance of emphasis on the country between the rivers Thames and Itchen, the reason is that it provided the first important road network of English history, so much of which was lost with the early decline of Winchester.

MAPS, ROAD GUIDES AND ROUTE BOOKS

Timperley, H. W. and Brill, Edith. *Ancient Trackways of Wessex.* Phoenix House, 1965.

Hippisley Cox, R. *The Green Roads of England,* 3rd edition. Methuen, 1927.

Codrington, T. *Roman Roads in Britain.* 2nd edition. SPCK, 1905.

Margary, I. D. *Roman Roads in Britain.* Phoenix House, 1955.

Good, R. *The Old Roads of Dorset.* 1st edition, Dorset Archaeological Society, 1940. 2nd edition, Commin, 1966.

Close, Sir Charles. *The Map of England.* Peter Davies, 1932.

Hawkes, C. F. C. 'Old Roads in Central Hampshire', *Hampshire Field Club and Archaeological Society Proceedings,* Vol 9, Part 3. 1925.

Rodney, Sir G. B. 'An Account of Alresford', *Hampshire Field Club Proceedings,* Vol 9, Part 3. 1925.

Box, E. G. 'Hampshire County Maps' etc, *Hampshire Field Club Proceedings,* Vol 12, Part 3. 1934.

The Lunway

Williams-Freeman, J. P. 'Short Cross-Valley Dykes on the Lunway', *Hampshire Field Club Proceedings*, Vol 13, Part 1. 1935.

See also (above) *Ancient Trackways of Wessex, Green Roads of England, Sketches of Hampshire*.

Ogilby, John. *Britannia*. 1675.

Senex, John. *Ogilby's Roads*, portable eidition. 1719.

Paterson's Roads. Guides to turnpikes in numerous editions from late 1700s, especially 18th edition, 1828.

Various smaller guides *c* 1800 by Leigh, Cary, etc.

The Gough Map of Great Britain. *c* 1360. Bodleian Library and Royal Geographical Society, 1958.

County maps without roads, late 1500s to early 1600s, by Speed, Saxton, Norden.

Large-scale county maps with roads:

Taylor, Isaac. *Hampshire*. 1759.

Milne, Thomas. *Hampshire*. 1791.

Taylor, Isaac. *Dorset*. 1765.

Rocque, Jonathan. *Berkshire*. *c* 1752–61.

Rocque, Jonathan. *Surrey*. *c* 1762–75.

Andrews, J. and Dury, A. *Wiltshire*. 1773.

Day and Masters. *Somerset*. 1782.

Numerous maps of the eighteenth and early nineteenth centuries on a smaller scale are available.

Ordnance Survey Manuscript Drawings. *c* 1795–1810.

Ordnance Survey period maps:

Iron Age (Southern Britain). 1962.

Roman Britain. 1956.

Britain in the Dark Ages. 1966.

Monastic Southern Britain. 1954.

A considerable amount of the evidence for early roads given in this book can still be found on the 1-inch Ordnance maps, though traces are often more numerous on issues prior to the current seventh series. Larger-scale Ordnance maps can be very rewarding on particular problems.

Biographical Notes

Cobbett, William. 1763–1835. Writer, politician, farmer with homes in Hampshire and Hampshire/Surrey border. Travelled widely through Wessex on horseback at a time when the turnpike system (which he avoided) was making a new pattern for main roads. *Rural Rides* published 1830.

Defoe, Daniel. 1660–1731. Born Foe. Businessman who turned to political writing and then novels. *Robinson Crusoe* was published in 1719. His *Tour of Great Britain* was composed towards the end of his life in 1724–6, and reflected earlier travels on horseback. The original edition (mostly pre-turnpike) is quoted in this book. Revised editions continued after his death.

Evelyn, John. 1620–1706. Diarist and friend of Charles II. Secretary Royal Society 1673. Travelled widely at home and in Europe, by carriage and horseback.

Fiennes, Celia. 1662–1741. Brought up on the Hampshire/Wiltshire border and travelled through Britain on horseback. The Wessex journeys recorded in her memoirs took place approximately in 1685–1702.

Gough, Richard. 1735–1809. Director of Society of Antiquaries 1771–97. Purchased at a sale the anonymous fourteenth-century map of Great Britain usually associated with his name, which he bequeathed to the Bodleian Library at Oxford.

Leland, John. 1506(?)–52. Became Antiquary to Henry VIII empowered to search records, etc, in cathedrals and monasteries. His itinerary covered the approximate period 1533–43 and was presumably made on horseback, though often gives the impression of walking.

Ogilby, John. 1600–76. A man of many talents who was appointed Charles II's Cartographer in 1666. His great work

Britannia Volume the First with its scroll maps of the main roads was made 1671–5. It was the first detailed survey of English and Welsh roads, many of which, of great antiquity, were to be abandoned and lost in the turnpike system that became general in the mid-1700s. The mileage, recorded on a hand-propelled wheel, was extremely accurate.

Paterson, Daniel. 1739–1825. Cartographer who became Assistant Quartermaster General to the Army. His first Route Book reflecting the new turnpike roads appeared in 1771 and successive editions were published till the eighteenth (1829) which continued with fresh maps showing the new railways at least till 1841.

Pepys, Samuel. 1633–1703. Naval administrator who maintained his diary till he was thirty-six when he ceased writing for fear of failing eyesight, though he never went blind. President Royal Society 1684. Travelled extensively in southern England, mostly by coach or carriage.

Stukeley, William. 1687–1765. Trained as a doctor (MD, Cambridge). Became antiquary and undertook notable work at Avebury and Stonehenge. One of the prime founders, and first secretary, of the Society of Antiquaries 1719. His tour of Great Britain, made on horseback mostly in 1723, provided records of Roman and other early roads.

Young, Arthur. 1741–1820. Agricultural writer who toured in Britain and Europe from 1767, noting farm practices which he published in book form. In southern England he used a light chaise and compared the state of the roads before and after the turnpikes were made.

INDEX

Index

Regional History and David & Charles Series

Railway Enthusiasts'
Series

These and other PAN books are obtainable
from all booksellers and newsagents. If you
have any difficulty please send purchase price
plus 7p postage to P.O. Box 11, Falmouth,
Cornwall.
While every effort is made to keep prices low,
it is sometimes necessary to increase prices at
short notice. PAN Books reserve the right to
show new retail prices on covers which may
differ from those advertised in the text or elsewhere.